11-16-47

George Bedigian
from
Ann Kolstad.

Book Sale
10/5/04

THE FIGHT OF
THE NORWEGIAN CHURCH
AGAINST NAZISM

THE MACMILLAN COMPANY
NEW YORK · BOSTON · CHICAGO · DALLAS
ATLANTA · SAN FRANCISCO

MACMILLAN AND CO., Limited
LONDON · BOMBAY · CALCUTTA · MADRAS
MELBOURNE

THE MACMILLAN COMPANY
OF CANADA, Limited
TORONTO

THE FIGHT OF
THE NORWEGIAN CHURCH
AGAINST NAZISM

by

BJARNE HÖYE

and

TRYGVE M. AGER

NEW YORK

THE MACMILLAN COMPANY

1943

CONTENTS

THE FIGHT OF
THE NORWEGIAN CHURCH
AGAINST NAZISM

CHAPTER I

THE NORWEGIANS UNITE

MILITARILY NORWAY was ill-prepared to meet the German surprise attack of April 9, 1940. Nevertheless the "blitz" was militarily more expensive than the aggressors had calculated. Politically and morally it has since become clear that they have suffered a defeat, because in these respects it can now safely be said that the Norwegian people were well prepared for attack.

There had always been strong cultural ties between Norway and Germany. In theology and ecclesiasticism the bonds between Norway and Luther's homeland have been strong. In 1930 more than 95 percent of the Norwegian people belonged to the State Church which is Evangelical Lutheran.

When on the morning of April 9th the Germans showered Norway with leaflets stating that they came as friends, they were probably entertaining the hope that they could use these age-old cultural and religious ties to bind Norway to the German scheme for world domination. But the leaflets fell unheeded. There were few who were deceived by them. The reason was exactly opposite to the one given by Reichskommissar Josef Terboven in his speech of September 25th when he found it opportune to begin seriously to nazify Norway, and appointed the quisling clique

1

to be his instrument. In his speech he tried to give the impression that the Norwegian people

were purposely prevented from understanding that great people in the centre of Europe. The mass of this people (the Norwegians) therefore knew little or nothing about the German people, its thoughts and feelings, its demand for life, its will to live and its great vital power. When this people then attached itself to National Socialism, the characterization of Nazi-Germany as an unnatural and unworthy system was accepted by Norwegians without consideration, and they made it their own opinion without independent examination.

Actually no political movement before or during the war has had so much publicity in Norway as Nazism, thanks to the vigorous propaganda conducted by the Nazis and to the "open door" policy of the Norwegian press. That the effect on the Norwegian people was negative is quite another point. The more the people learned about Nazism and its insatiable "demand for life," and the more they saw its teachings practiced on the German people and their neighbours, the stronger grew the hostility towards the Nazi system and all it implied. There had originally been some more or less well-based sympathy for the Germans which had found expression during the last war in the temporary adoption of starving Viennese children. This sympathy was exploited by the Nazis in their propaganda against the Versailles Treaty, but it was also given its death blow by the Nazis when they revealed their true character in words and deeds.

The Nazi treatment of the Church and of religious and ethical values had perhaps the strongest effect. At one phase in their struggle for power in Germany the Nazis had tried to bewilder the people and conceal their true aims by unfurling a banner against corruption and immorality and for the re-establishment of Christian morals among the people. This propaganda achieved some initial success, even among serious Christians in Norway. Men who felt acutely the dangers of loose liberalism in the ethical, religious, and moral spheres, were naturally attracted by a system which promised to reinstate order, sobriety, and authority.

Long before Europe was set on fire a large part of the Norwegian people were tense spectators of the remarkable religious war which was being waged in Hitler's Germany. The picture became steadily clearer despite all the Nazi authorities could do to hide the actual facts and the significance of the struggle. An unprincipled and heathen power was trying to win the soul of the German people so as to mould it and direct it for Nazi purposes without hindrance from the Christian Church or from the dictates of conscience. All authority and influence, except that of the State, was systematically abolished, preferably by destruction from within, by maneuvers with fifth columnists of all kinds, by establishing an ecclesiastical "Quisling Party" like the "German Christians" and using it as a lever against the Confessional Church, by flirting with German paganism and the worship of Blut and Boden, by taking away the children and young people from the influence of their parents and the Church and systematically hammering in the new Nazi state-worship, by bullying and terrorizing the clergy into obedience and in an emergency putting the obstinate into prisons and concentration camps—as in the case of Pastor Niemöller—and by enticing out all the evil instincts, making the Church an accomplice in anti-Semitism, racial hatred and other crimes.

The Norwegian public was kept well informed of the perverse developments in Hitler-Germany by telegrams in the press, by newspaper commentaries, books, articles, discussions, and lectures. Leading Christians such as the well-known author, Ronald Fangen, visited Germany and wrote and spoke from their own experiences against the growing danger of Nazism to the fundamental Christian values of the people. The people became so well informed both politically and religiously that even Norway's tiny Nazi Party, Nasjonal Samling, found it wisest from a propagandist point of view to deny too close a relationship with German Nazism.

The Norwegian people were, therefore, already well acquainted with the Nazis when they came in the dead of night on April 9th and scattered their mixture of bombs and assurances of friendship over Norway. At first the "blitz" seemed a knock-out blow. But then Hitler was good enough to set up Quisling as Norwegian "Leader" and Gauleiter. This had the effect of a bucket of cold water and brought the people to their senses after the first stunning blows of the totally unexpected attack. The King, Government, and Parliament were able to escape northwards and saved what was necessary for a constitutional continuation of the fight for the country's freedom and independence on British soil. Below will be told something of the part played by the ecclesiastical and religious front in this fight. It is one of the most interesting phases because here the main struggle has been waged and is being waged for the soul of the Norwegian people. Here Nazism has had to fall back defeated time and time again, after its many assaults from every possible angle. The Church has certainly not conducted a spiritless defensive struggle. The struggle has been conducted actively, wisely and fearlessly on the full and firm foundations of the Christian faith.

The Calm Before the Storm

In the very first days of the war the Quisling regime produced chaotic conditions in the administration on account of the spontaneous and united opposition of the people to the quisling traitors and their "Nasjonal Samling" (i.e., "National Union") party. The war in Norway was creating many difficulties for the Germans at that time, and what they desired above all else in the part of Norway which they had occupied, was law and order. They, therefore, decided that it was wisest to put Quisling and his little gang back in the box until another occasion, after only seven days "rule," and established instead the so-called Administrative Council composed of well-known and honorable Norwegians. Through this Council Norway was ensured a fair measure of self-government with a minimum of interference from the occupation authorities.

The Church also benefitted from the period of non-interference which now followed. Reichskommissar Terboven promised to respect the decisions of the Hague Convention regarding full religious freedom in the occupied regions. The German soldiers were instructed to behave well and considerately towards the civil population, and it must be said in the interests of truth that these instructions were on the whole followed and carried through with good discipline outside the actual battle-zones during those first weeks of the occupation.

All this should have had a very reassuring effect. The Germans tried to show that they were not as bad as they were made out to be, and that they were misrepresented and libeled by English propaganda. But this apparent idyll was disturbed by certain deeper currents which showed that this was but a calm before the storm, that it was only a part of established Nazi tactics, to further their policy of aggression alternately by pacific means and by terror, alternately by pacts of friendship and by assault. For the moment it was wisest to deal carefully with the Norwegian people and to exploit the possibilities of "co-operation" to the utmost extent.

In the days immediately following the April 9th attack it was privately admitted in German quarters that the intention was to nazify Norway as quickly as possible. There was no reason to think that these Nazi plans had been put away for good, even though the quislings had been disposed of. This was shown with ever-growing clarity by the secret political negotiations between the Germans and the representatives of the Norwegian Parliament. The Church also began to feel that it was working on an insecure foundation, and the Church's Primate, Bishop Eivind Berggrav, soon found himself in a very dangerous position.

Long before the outbreak of war in 1939 Bishop Berg-

grav had worked positively and actively for a policy of
reconciliation between the peoples. He had done so in
writing and speeches and by personal conversations with
politicians in many countries, including Lord Halifax and
Field Marshal Goering. As President of the World Al-
liance for the Promotion of Friendship through the
Churches, he gained a worldwide reputation as a Christian, a man of learning and, above all, a man of peace. He
continued his work for the Christian spirit against the
spirit of hate after Hitler's attack on Poland.

When eventually Norway was invaded, Berggrav still
worked in the same spirit to help, relieve, and reconcile.
Whole-heartedly he set about his new tasks. He became
misunderstood because of his work—not least because of a
radio appeal to Norwegian guerilla fighters. The circumstances are not entirely clear, but two things at least seem
certain: Berggrav's whole-hearted and unfailing patriotism; and the Nazis' attempt to undermine his position and
separate him from his compatriots. In the first few weeks
of the occupation the Nazis began to use the Oslo radio to
spread false rumours about Berggrav. Pictures were published in the Nazi press which were intended to compromise him in the eyes of the public. A slogan was circulated
which said: "Let us follow our leaders, Quisling, Hamsun,
and Berggrav."

The object was clear. By sowing doubt and disseminat-
ing falsehoods about the leader of the Church, the Nazis
hoped to create dissension and bewilderment within the
Church itself, and thus compromise it and render it in-
capable of offering any kind of effective resistance to the

coming nazification and deprivation of its authority. It almost looked as if this plot against Bishop Berggrav and the Church would be successful. Many hard words were spoken about the Bishop both at home and abroad. A weaker personality than Bishop Berggrav might have given up and might have remained caught in the insidious trap. But Berggrav learned much from those first contacts with the Nazi system—he learned about the subtlety of the snake as well as the gentleness of the dove. His shining, open, and active personality has gained more prophetic depth and clarity of vision without losing its frankness. He became a true leader of the Church who will occupy a prominent place when the history of Norway's hour of affliction comes to be written.

The Church Orders General Mobilization

On September 25, 1940, the Germans decided that the time had come to break the political lull and to enter seriously upon the nazification of Norway. This process would involve a complete revolution, not only politically by the establishment of a branch of the Berlin dictatorship, but also by pulling up by the roots the very foundations of Norwegian life and culture. On that day Terboven "deposed" the King and Government and dissolved the political parties, and at one blow the Church had been drawn into the immediate danger-zone. Christians in Norway were already on guard, and they were not slow in appreciating the situation. Something extraordinary in the history of the Church then occurred, something which can best be likened to a general mobilization. In the hour of danger the Norwegian Christians were welded together in a single firm block.

This was publicly manifested on October 28, 1940, during a meeting in Oslo's largest public hall, Calmeyer Street Mission House. This was roughly one month after Nazism's "New Era" had been inaugurated by the formation of the quislingist shadow-government, composed of so-called "commissarial councillors" under German control. At this meeting the *Christian Council for Joint Deliberation* (Kristent Samraad) was formed.

It was strongly emphasized in the report concerning the new council, read by Hans Höegh, deputy chairman of the Oslo bishopric council, that it was not a question of founding a new body with organizational authority. It was in reality nothing other than a forward movement of the whole active Christian front in Norway. Christian unity thus came into the light of day in quite a new way. All clerical divisions and "party politics" were swept aside in face of the common danger from without. The whole action was prepared and carried out without fuss and its potentialities were at first not generally realized. But it was of incalculable significance for the morale and for the spirit of resistance of the Norwegian people in the days that followed. The active Christian front had cleared its decks for action. Calm and united on the old yet evernew foundations of the Gospel, they stood ready for battle.

It was announced at the meeting in Calmeyer Street Mission House that "Christian deliberation on behalf of the Norwegian Church" would take place between the following: Bishop Berggrav, Professor Hallesby, Ludvig

Hope, Kristian Hansson, Hans Höegh (school governor), the Rev. R. Indrebö, the Rev. Ingvald B. Carlsen and Einar Smebye (mission chaplain). The proclamation was signed by eighteen of the leading men of the Norwegian Church, including the seven bishops. Those who know something of Norwegian Church affairs and of the religious disputes which have gone on for years, will always regard this reunion of leaders of different theological tendencies as something of a miracle. This was expressed in the four speeches held at the meeting, and it supplies proof of both the breadth and the depth of the united front.

Professor O. Hallesby's speech underscored the deep feeling of a country and people under the great hand of God. He also gave expression to the urge felt by all Christian Norwegians to serve their war-ravaged country and their unfortunate fellow-citizens. He pointed out that God had also promised to give the people their *rights,* and he ended by expressing his joy that the newly formed Christian union had not been built on compromise but on the ancient foundations of faith.

The speech of Bishop J. Stören seemed to be an octave higher than Hallesby's. Its subject was loyalty, loyalty to the ancient Christianity and the obligation to carry on the work of the Kingdom of God. This basic theme inspired the well-known lay speaker, Ludvig Hope, to speak in an even more cheerful key about "Our Christian Heritage." With burning enthusiasm he described the value of this Christian heritage, that it was worth sacrifice and suffering, that it was not the time to lose courage nor to fail, but to fight determinedly and fearlessly for everything men held dear. Bishop Berggrav struck the final chord in a characteristic speech on "open-heartedness," the open-heartedness which in full and unconditional surrender to God is strong and confident through dark days and full of God's peace when in the fray. The Bishop's speech was like a bright fanfare before entering the lists against the pagan powers seeking to mould all mankind to the Nazi pattern:

God's kingdom in our country, that is the country's future. God made us Norwegian just as he gave you and me our own special peculiarities, our own special dispositions. It is in your soul that God meets you. He will not put you in uniform and destroy your individuality. He will save you and liberate you. Thus is Norway created by Him, and thus will He save Norway and make the Norwegians a medium for His song of open-heartedness the world over.

We stand together now. All Christians in this land are now facing in the same direction: Help comes from God. From God we get our open-heartedness, enabling us to live, work, pray, and hold out in a compact of good conscience.

All Christians in Norway facing in the same direction in a united front—that was the masterpiece which was accomplished in those October days only a month after Germany had thrown down the political gauntlet to the Norwegian people. They had the privilege of forming the first front in the Norwegian civil population's stubborn and glorious fight against the foreign oppressors. The sports front and many others were later to follow the example of the Church. The Christian front was not only the first, but perhaps also the most broadly based of the various fronts formed in the fight for freedom. It stood then, and has stood ever since, firmly rooted in two fundamentals: The Bible and the Constitution. The quisling, Arne Rydland, spoke truly when he said in the middle of 1941 that "the Christian front is the most difficult to conquer."

CHAPTER II

THE FIRST CHALLENGE BY THE
NEW REGIME

IT WAS NOT long before the Church received its first challenge from the new rulers. They demanded that an alteration should be made in the Common Prayer of the service-book. The paragraph in the prayer referring to the King, Parliament, and Government was to be taken out, and a prayer for the new Nazi authorities was to be inserted. The demand was a logical result of the German decree which declared that these keystones of the Norwegian constitution had been abolished. But this demand was not simply humiliating for the Norwegian people from a political point of view. King Haakon and Crown Prince Olav had won a permanent place in the hearts of the people by their brave leadership of the people when under attack by German bombers. The King had become the symbol for the Norwegian will for freedom, and all hopes for victory and restoration rested in him. Never had the people prayed so fervently for their King and Royal Family as they did during that dark hour. The demand to alter the Common Prayer, therefore, seemed like a blow against life itself. Bishop Berggrav said "No" on behalf of the Church when the demand was first made.

It appears from the information that is available that the

Nazi authorities at the same time made another demand—to take over the control of the religious programs that were broadcast. The Church had at that time a special program committee led by Pastor Ingvald B. Carlsen, which directed religious broadcasts, and which had operated to the satisfaction of everyone except the Nazis. Searching systematically for every key position in the national and cultural life of the country, the Nazis had planned to take over the religious broadcasting program as a first blow against the Church.

The Church chose to submit to some extent to the first demand. It did not consider it expedient to come to blows with its opponent over the Common Prayer. It could afford to wait. Reports indicate that a compromise was arranged. The Church accepted the deletion from the Common Prayer, but firmly refused to accept any prayer for the Quisling regime; and the authorities dropped their demands for the nazification of the religious broadcasts. But the alterations to the Common Prayer caused sorrow and opposition in congregations everywhere.

Certain ministers continued to read the prayer unaltered. Others stopped reading when they reached the omitted paragraph, and the congregation would then recite the prayer for the Royal Family, Parliament, and Government. In the homes, too, the Common Prayer was read aloud in its entirety. In a little town in West Norway a five-year-old girl had been to church one Sunday and came home very disappointed. She complained that the minister had forgotten to read "the part about the King that father used to read." The alteration of the prayer had a psychological effect which was quite the reverse to what was intended, because the thoughts and prayers of the people were drawn more strongly than ever before to King Haakon.

Several events gave cause for vigilance and warned of an approaching era of persecution. First came the arrest of Ronald Fangen, the author and Christian leader. The cause of his arrest was at first believed to be an article in the October number of Bishop Berggrav's journal, *For Church and Culture*. The article was entitled "On Loyalty," and Fangen quoted here the German historian Fichte in order to show how one should be loyal to one's people. Fichte's description of the position of Prussia under Napoleon a hundred years ago, described almost word for word the position of the Norwegian people under German rule today:

We are conquered, but whether we shall also be justly despised, whether we shall add the loss of our honour to all our other losses, depends in the future on ourselves. The battle of arms is over; the new battle depends on principles, morals, character. Let us give our guests (the French) a picture of loyalty towards country and friends, of incorruptible uprightness and respect for duty, which they can take with them as a friendly gift when they eventually return home. Let us take care that they do not despise us. Nothing is more likely to provoke contempt than our fearing them in an exaggerated way or our giving up our own way of life and exerting ourselves to imitate theirs.

In 1807 Fichte was allowed to speak such words to his compatriots without being harmed. In 1940 Fangen was thrown into prison because he allowed the words of a German patriot once again to arouse a people which this time was oppressed by the Germans. The arrest of Ronald Fangen caused a tremendous sensation all over Scandinavia. The Oxford Group Movement was banned at the same time because Fangen was connected with it, and because it was altogether too reminiscent of that abomination which the Nazis call "English sickness." Fangen became ill during his stay in prison. It has been said that his illness was caused by various forms of direct torture, but this does not appear to be true. He was transferred to a hospital and eventually released in the summer of 1941, just before Hitler began his "Crusade" against the Soviet Union and demanded "Crusaders" from every country.

The case of Fangen showed that freedom of conscience and personal security were endangered, in spite of all Terboven's assurances not to interfere with the freedom of religion and the independence of the courts of justice. Towards the close of the first year of occupation followed a number of episodes and decrees which demonstrated anew the worthlessness of Nazi promises. First came the attack against the actual constitutional system of justice in the country. On November 14th the Nazi "Department of Justice" issued a decree which gave the Nazi regime authority to direct the composition of the courts as they pleased, in contradiction of the principles on which the Norwegian courts are based. The Ministry was empowered to dismiss and appoint mediators and to sweep away the chosen jurymen, judges, and experts, and to appoint others. The Supreme Court emphatically pointed out to the "Department of Justice" that the independence of the Courts was established in the Constitution, and that it was also recognized by Reichskommissar Terboven on September 28, 1940, in accordance with international law. If the decree were enforced, said the Supreme Court justices, the results would be fatal for Norwegian law and justice. In spite of this warning the decree was passed and put into practice, with the result that all the members of the Supreme Court resigned from their offices.

The destruction by the Nazis of the thousand-year-old Norwegian law-state, and the "New Order's" return to the barbarism of old, were being demonstrated at that time by a number of assaults by the Hird. This band of young quisling Storm Troopers began to operate in exactly the same way as the Hitler S.A. gangs had done in the early days of the Nazi struggle in Germany, in order to excite and terrorize, and to turn up-side-down all that belonged to the old way of life. On November 30th the Hird forced its way into a class room of the Oslo School of Business. According to a written report from the school's Association of Teachers the Hird attacked pupils and ill-treated them in the presence of the teachers. As weapons they used chairs and tables made of iron which were thrown at the students. One member of the Hird also used a club. The teacher in charge of the class was struck down, and the school's headmaster, its inspector, and yet another teacher were also attacked and struck, receiving quite serious wounds.

On December 11th a 16-year-old apprentice, Gunnar Stabel, was kidnapped in Oslo Town Hall and taken to the Hird Home in Björn Farmann Street in a car. Here he was taken down in the cellar, where a Hird-man questioned him and gave him ten to fifteen lashes with his belt. The reason why this boy was abducted and beaten appears to have been that he had been observed a few days earlier with a paper clip in the lapel of his jacket, which was then a popularly accepted emblem of national solidarity and an expression for the hope that Norway should once more be free.

As a third instance of officially recorded brutality by the Hird may be mentioned the attack on Holterman, chairman of the Trondheim Student Association, on November 29, 1940. A Hird detachment entered the Association's premises and asked Holterman whether he was willing to put up certain placards for the Quisling party. Holterman refused. The Hird leader then ordered him to be thrashed. He was struck in the face so that he fell down. When he got on his feet again the Hird leader repeated his question, but Holterman refused again, and once more he was struck to the ground. The Hird leader eventually summoned his men, and they drove off.

These attacks made the deepest impression because they apparently were committed with the full approval of the authorities. The ruffians, despite being reported, were never brought before a court of law. As a matter of fact the "Minister for Police," Jonas Lie, on December 14th issued a circular to the police, which strongly advised them to join the "party in power," Nasjonal Samling. It also stated that:

The Hirdmen are Nasjonal Samling's political soldiers and must be strongly supported in their fight to establish the ideas of N. S. A good relationship and a good cooperation must be established between the police and the Hird. It must, of course, never happen that a Hirdman is arrested unless he commits a *crime*.

It was quite clear that the new quisling rulers intended to impose the New Order on the Norwegian community in record time, according to German pattern and on German initiative. The political "clean-up" which took place during the winter of 1940–41 was apparently not only an attempt to destroy the long-established Norwegian State, but was also an attempt to destroy the political conscience of all servants and officials of the State. The clergy's oath of silence, a pledge treasured by the Church, and with justice called "The Magna Carta of the Conscience," was also attacked. The "Ministry of Police" issued one day a decree which cancelled the clergy's oath of silence in cases where the police so required it, and the pastors were threatened with imprisonment if they contravened the order. A series of similar decrees were rushed out in "blitz" fashion at the height of the Christmas season. It was certainly done with the tactical intent of sweeping the Norwegian nation off its feet before it had time to collect itself and to realize what was actually happening. It was a kind of 9th of April on the inner front.

It was here that the Supreme Court, to its everlasting glory, clear-sightedly and bravely met the danger in the only way it could under the prevailing conditions. It resigned, as mentioned above, in protest against the destruction of law and justice, and thus made the violation plain both for Norwegians and the whole world. By its action the Supreme Court also helped to pave the way for the great counter-offensive by the Church against Nazism. All Christians were mobilized. They only waited for the order to attack. The attack came in the beginning of 1941 and it was so superbly prepared and conducted and so overwhelming in its force that the Nazis in Norway have subsequently never been able to overcome the effects of their defeat. It was in those days that the hate felt by the quislings and their chief organ, *Fritt Folk,* towards the leaders of the Church began to find open expression.

CHAPTER III

THE CHURCH ATTACKS

THE CHURCH OFFENSIVE was begun on January 15, 1941, by a letter to the Nazi Minister of Church and Education, Ragnar Skancke, signed by all the seven bishops of Norway. The letter had a quiet, dignified tone which effectively re-inforced the power of the attack. It was later to echo over the whole free world as a clear and fearless indictment of Nazism. The bishops' letter began by clarifying the position of the State Church in relation to the State by establishing it on the foundation of justice and the Articles of Faith:

The very foundation of the Church of Norway rests on a definite constitutional relationship to the State, and on the assumption that the duty of the State and all departments of the government is to uphold righteousness and justice in accordance with the will of God. The Norwegian Constitution states: "The Evangelical Lutheran religion shall be the official religion of Norway." It therefore is imperative and essential that the Church should know clearly whether the State, which is also concerned with ecclesiastical matters, accepts and honours the legal and moral obligations contained in the Church's Articles of Faith and in the Bible.

The bishops also mentioned the promises, which the Nazi authorities had made since April 9th to respect law and justice and full religious freedom, and they continued:

Recently, however, much serious doubt has arisen concerning the validity of the statements made by the bishops to their church members. We are faced with the problem of whether the State and its departments will maintain order and justice as provided by our Church's Articles of Faith.

We point to three specific instances which, in substance are interwoven and which bear out the contention that acts of violence, instead of being prevented, are actually condoned, and that there are signs that the fundamental principles of justice have been broken down.

The bishops then enumerated some of the concrete causes for the unrest: The systematic rule of terror by the Hird, next the joint resignation of the Supreme Court, and, last but not least, the interference with the ministers' pledge of silence. These accusations were supported by documentary evidence, and brief resumes were also given.

Regarding the behaviour of the Hird it was pointed out that the revolting nature of the single acts of violence was such as to make them a threat to the security of society as a whole, particularly in view of the fact that the highest representative of law and order (the Nazi Minister of Police, Jonas Lie) on December 14th instructed the police not to interfere but to give "active support to the Hird." The bishops also pointed out the widespread sense of insecurity which was created with regard to the foundations of law and order after the members of the Supreme Court found themselves obliged to resign their duties:

Since in the Articles of Faith (Augustana, Paragraph 16) the Church upholds that which is legitimate in the State's actions, and since these articles call upon every Christian to be loyal to the State, and the acting head of the Department of Church and Education will certainly agree that it is the duty and the right of Church officials to speak up and request information on such series matters as those just mentioned.

He will also understand that the seriousness of the situation will not diminish when we emphasize that violence and that a spirit of hate is developing among the people. Not the least important is the way such things affect growing youth. The training of Christian character is by law assigned to church and school, and this constitutes one of the Church's main tasks. Therefore, when the Department of Church and Education, in a bulletin dated November 12th and addressed to all school officials, advises all responsible schoolmen to guarantee upon their honour that they will give positive and active support to every resolution and decree issued by the new authorities—then, we view the whole matter as approaching a conflict of conscience in the very essence of our profession.

With regard to the degree by the Nazi Ministry of Police concerning the abolition of the ministers' oath of silence, the letter from the bishops stressed that the oath of silence was not simply established by law, but had always been a fundamental requirement in the ecclesiastical calling for ministering to sorrow and receiving confessions from people in trouble. They declared it was of the utmost importance to the Church that people should have full and unqualified confidence in the clerical oath of silence, such as it had been recognized both in Norwegian law and in the Church's decrees throughout all times and in all Christian lands. To abolish this Magna Carta of the conscience, said the bishops, would be to attack the very heart of the Church, an attack which took on an especially serious character by the fact that Paragraph 5 authorized police to imprison an offending minister and force him to talk without his being taken before a court of law.

"Minister" Skancke tried at first to take the easy course of not replying to the bishops' letter, and let it disappear in the flow of official correspondence. But this was not what the Church had planned. Having waited a few weeks three of the bishops—Berggrav, Stören, and Maroni—instructed by their colleagues, obtained an interview with Skancke in order to emphasize the serious nature of the letter and to ask when they might expect a reply.

Something happened during this personal interview which the Nazis had expected least of all. The bishops produced a document which with Lutheran fearlessness and illuminating clarity drew the demarcation line between the zones of authority of the Church and State, and sounded a blunt warning to the Nazi authorities:

It is useless to try to dismiss the Church by saying that it is mixing into politics. Luther truly says: "The Church is not interfering in worldly affairs when it exhorts the authorities to be obedient to the highest authority which is God." When the leaders of the community permit violence and practice injustice and coerce the soul, then the Church is the guardian of the soul. A human soul is more important than the whole world. . . . With all its human weaknesses the Church is authorized by God to teach His law and His gospel to all people. Therefore the Church can never remain silent where God's word is ignored and where sin arises. In this the Church is adamant and can not in these essentials be bound by any government.

We therefore exhort the heads of the community to end all which conflicts with God's holy arrangements regarding justice, truth, freedom of conscience and goodness and to build entirely on God's law of living.

Three days later a reply was received from Skancke dated February 1, 1941. The hope was expressed that the Church and its men would have confidence in Nasjonal Samling when it was repeated that no interference with the Church was contemplated. The letter also contained some words to the effect that Nasjonal Samling's motto was "order, justice and peace," and that it was the intention of the existing government to see that this motto was practiced throughout the country as far as possible. The allegedly concrete instances would be investigated, wrote Skancke. (Nothing has been heard since of the results of these promised investigations.) The reply was altogether just talk and evasion. Only on one single point was an attempt made to counter the bishops' statement, namely in regard to the decree issued by the Ministry of Police about the pastors' oath of silence. The Minister of Church and Education tried to defend it by saying that the oath of silence had not been absolute before and that the decree only meant a new reservation. All these twisted phrases ended characteristically enough with the following open threat:

The Church is not the only institution in need of peace to fulfill its mission; the State itself needs it. We hereby most sincerely warn the Church against any acts which may increase the unrest of our people. Thoughtless action now may result in serious consequences for the Church. Now as before the Church needs the State in order to be a true Church of the people, and the State needs the Church to maintain law and order and peace. The State and the Church must stand together and serve the people which they lead. We therefore ask the bishops of the Church and through them all the ministers of the Church of Norway to act in a spirit of good will so that this cooperation may succeed. May I at the same time request that circular letters from the bishops to ministers or congregations be forwarded in three copies to the Department of Church and Education.

This reply exemplified all the typical traits of Nazism: Empty assurances and soothing phrases unrelated to reality; no proper attempt to meet the allegations, but a resort to threats in order to get "troublesome elements" to keep quiet and "helpful"—quiet, at least, so that it all might die away and be forgotten. But this time the Nazis underestimated the strength and determination of the forces which had been set in motion. Regardless of the threats, the Church went immediately into action, by-passing the Nazi authorities. The action can almost be regarded as a revolution. The bishops approached the Norwegian congregations directly by means of a Pastoral Letter, and frankly and fearlessly explained the *whole* affair. It was requested that the contents of the Pastoral Letter should be made known to the congregations in the best possible way.

The Church's action received immediate support from a number of important Christian organizations, and from creeds of faith other than the State Church. They were the Norwegian Lutheran Home Mission, the Norwegian Sunday School League, the Western Home Mission, the Norwegian Foreign Mission, Norway's Finnmark Mission, The Norwegian Seamen's Mission, the Santal Mission,

Norway's Christian Youth League, the Norwegian Lutheran China Mission, the Salvation Army, the Congress of Dissenting Faiths, and the Philadelphia Congregation in Oslo.

It seemed as if a flood has been released against the Nazi authorities. They tried to dam the flow with the help of the police and all the powers they could summon. They tried to prevent the reading of the Pastoral Letter to congregations. The Norwegian Church Association of Ministers had risen in support of the bishops and had agreed to pray for the latter on February 16th, the Sunday when the Pastoral Letter was to be read to the congregations. On February 14th the Chairman of the Association received a telegram from Skancke which expressly prohibited such a prayer. The Association's committee met hastily in Oslo and decided unanimously not to yield to Skancke's "request." The new Nazi secretary of the Department of Church and Education, Sigmund Feyling, was summoned by the committee and asked to explain why and on what grounds the prohibition had been issued. He had some difficulty in replying to these questions but it appeared from the conversation that he had twice approached Skancke to advise him not to send the telegram, but in vain. Finally Feyling declared that if the clergy used the prayer in spite of the prohibition, it would create unrest among the people. The committee replied that this unrest already existed and that it was created not by the clergy but by others, meaning the Nazis. The next day Feyling conferred again with Skancke and the result was that Skancke capitulated. The prohibition was to be regarded as never having been issued, and the prayer for the bishops was delivered the next day in all the churches in the land. Thus on this point the Nazi authorities were driven back after having tried to interfere in the internal affairs of the Church.

On February 11th, however, the Department of Church and Education had sent the clergy a warning prohibiting them from reading the Pastoral Letter to their congregations. It was found impossible to get this prohibition repealed, and the Church thereupon received a foretaste of what a Nazi police rule is like. In many places the police entered the churches in order to frighten the clergy from reading the Letter in spite of the prohibition. One incident caused deep indignation all over North Norway. While Bishop Krohn-Hansen was giving his sermon in Tromsö, two uniformed German soldiers marched into the church, seized the Bishop's wife and took her outside. She was then interrogated and asked whether the Bishop intended to read the Pastoral Letter to the congregation. She replied that she did not know. She was then allowed to re-enter the church, having been told that she would be arrested if the Letter were read. The two military police followed her into the church and did not leave until the end of the service when the Letter had not been read.

Nevertheless, the Germans and their quisling helpers failed to muffle the voice of the Church. Despite the police the Letter was made known to the congregations from the majority of the Church pulpits. The Church also had it printed and spread all over the country. The authorities stepped in again and tried to confiscate some of the 50,000 copies. Again the Church protested, declaring that the authorities were unlawfully interfering with the Church's right to keep in contact with congregations. The arm of the law proved itself to be too short, and most of the printed copies had soon spread over the country. Also "illegal" editions were printed and, via a hundred secret channels, the Pastoral Letter was distributed to the whole people. The police raided all the printing plants in Oslo on February 17th in order to find the printers responsible, but the authorities were defeated, and remained defeated.

The action of the Norwegian Church has been justly described as "the most crushing indictment of totalitarian methods, of broken promises and destruction of Christian rights and values that has ever been made by the Protestant Church within the German sphere of influence."

The Strength of the Church

The strength of the Church in this first clash with the Nazis lay in the fact that it concentrated on the essentials, and stood on a foundation of justice and a clear conscience. It was, therefore, able to speak with full authority. The bishops pointed out clearly and plainly the demarcation line between lawful regulation and anarchy. In a noteworthy speech to the Legal Association in Oslo on "Religion and Justice," Bishop Berggrav, February 15, 1941, explained the judicial foundations of the struggle:

When the truth becomes something sacred for us, it is then that it can create martyrs. It is only when a cause becomes sacred to a man that it becomes a driving force inside him so that nothing becomes impossible for him. The same is true of what we call society. A society cannot survive only by rational causes. Take away the holy sense of duty, and only millions of legal paragraphs remain. They multiply to billions of new laws, and yet society falls asunder.

The Church submits to the law. The Church has no powers of jurisdiction. Mark well: *Submits to the law*; that does not mean to *every apparently legal innovation*. Because above all laws and above all power stands God, in the way that His Word speaks to our conscience.

The Church which speaks and acts, filled with this sacred inner sense of duty and obligation, possesses the vitality and invincibility of the martyr church, said Berggrav. It carries within itself its own victory in the face of what ordinary mortals would call certain defeat.

The Nazi authorities had to make a difficult choice: either to try to smash the Church's resistance by brute force, and thus convert it to a martyr Church; or to make a temporary withdrawal, and hope to undermine the Church gradually by wiles and cunning artifice. They chose the latter course, and tried to cover their retreat with a smoke screen of speeches and articles by a few quisling clerics.

Most typical was the broadcast by Feyling, the dean from Egersund, who had been promoted to secretary of the Department of Church and Education because of his faith in the New Order. At the end of February he appealed to the clergy on behalf of the Department. His subject was "The Norwegian Church and the Norwegian People." The speech was largely a dose of soothing syrup, composed of reassuring words and "nice" religious expressions: "To take the Church from the people would be to break a 900-year-old tradition and would deprive our people of the most valuable of all constructive forces. Therefore, Nasjonal Samling has said that the basic values of Christianity must be safeguarded. . . . The present government is imbued with the spirit of Augustine. . . . There is no more reason to talk about a Church struggle than to talk about a general persecution." In other words, Feyling tried to convince the people that the bishops were being unduly alarmed and that the Holy Sepulchre was safe with the new rulers. At one point in his speech, however, he betrayed the anxiety being felt by the authorities over developments on the Church front:

But then there are many who say: "We would like to go to church during these times," and do so, too, but we often leave hurt and depressed. Many ministers talk in a way which makes it all heavy and sad. They talk as if an era of persecution is impending in our land. And this can only mean that these ministers cherish mistrust and ill-will towards the authorities.

Some notice must be taken of such remarks. The Ministry has recently received a number of letters which give expression to these complaints. On February 11th the Ministry sent a circular to the clergy asking them to take every possible care when preaching and in their general conduct.

Minister Skancke had not succeeded in getting the "peace" which he wanted and had tried to achieve by threats and orders. The clergy had not taken "every possible care." That much was clear from Mr. Feyling's speech.

The Church Boycotts the Radio

Even though the Nazis now had to proceed more carefully, they never forgot their goal and tried to attain it by
various means. It was not long before they turned their
attention once more to the religious broadcasts, which they
were determined to bring into conformity with the New
Order. In the beginning of March, 1941, Skancke decided
that the religious part of the radio programs should be
transferred to Propaganda Chief Gulbrand Lunde's Department of Culture, where a special office was set up to
be run by Feyling. All religious material was to be censored and approved by this office, so as to ensure that it
was written in the "new spirit."

This arrangement brought the Nazis no pleasure. All
they succeeded in doing was to isolate themselves even
more from 99 per cent of the Norwegian people. Pastor
Carlsen declared at once that he would no longer have
anything to do with the religious broadcasts under the
new arrangement. The whole affair was discussed at a
large meeting of clergy in Oslo. The consequence was a
very effective boycott of the radio by the clergy. Except for
a handful of Nazi clergymen, not a single minister was
afterwards to be heard on the official, Nazi-controlled
Oslo radio. It was all accomplished by a tacit understanding. Every minister was expected to act in accordance with
his beliefs, true to the maxim: "Keep your heart warm
and your head cool."

In face of this boycott the Nazi authorities were practically helpless. In a circular to ministers and congrega-

tional councils on April 5th the authorities tried to break the boycott, partly by persuasion, partly by the demand to be allowed to broadcast church services, and partly by the threat to abolish all religious broadcasts. The bishops replied on behalf of the Church that the State itself was to blame for all difficulty through having discontinued the earlier arrangement whereby services and prayers were broadcast, an arrangement which had the full support of the Church. The arrangement of religious broadcasts had now been taken over by the State, and according to the circular there was no clear distinction between State and political party. The bishops wrote:

Each individual must act in accordance with his beliefs, and have regard to the Church's responsibility to preach the Gospel to all peoples, and to protect this work from every combination with worldly partisan tendencies which would be untenable from a Christian point of view.

The ministers themselves decide whether they will broadcast and speak outside their Church and congregation. The congregation's services are the congregation's own. It is therefore a matter of choice whether services are made available to a larger public or not. All that matters is that the Word shall live pure and free. This does not only demand that the speaker is spiritually free, but also that the listeners hear the Word under conditions and circumstances which do not weaken the spirit and true purpose of the Word.

Opinion has always differed on the question whether the radio has been a gain or a loss for the Church. The Word of God lived in this land before the radio arrived. It did not always reach so many, but it may perhaps have made a greater impression. The Church can therefore not make any decisive objections of principle when the Ministry speaks of the possibility that the religious broadcasts may have to be discontinued.

The main thing will always be that the Church and all Christian communities are free, as established by international law, to teach the full Word of God within the congregations.

The Nazi authorities never succeeded in breaking this boycott of the radio by the Church. The Nazi-controlled "Norwegian State Broadcasting" was at the same time effectively boycotted by the Norwegian people, both by listeners and performers. There arose the anomaly that the number of radio listeners' licenses increased at the same time as the number of listeners and performers fell. The explanation was that people secured licenses to maintain radio receiving sets in order to listen to the Norwegian broadcasts from London and other free stations. "Norwegian State Broadcasting" became a ghost, a shadow which was virtually erased even before the state of emergency in September, 1941, when the Germans confiscated all radio sets in Norway. Because of the unity and strength of the Norwegian people, the radio, one of the most dangerous means by which to poison the people's soul, was knocked out of Nazis' hands and used against them. Here, too, church men played an important part, acting wisely and fearlessly.

The Church Refuses to Be Rendered "Harmless"

One or two aspects of the radio dispute are worthy of note. First, the Department of Church and Education approached the clergy and congregational councils directly by means of a circular letter instead of taking the normal, lawful course through the bishops. This must be regarded as an attempt to avoid the united Church front in order to

capture single individuals who might be weaker or less
clear-minded. It was, in fact, an attempt to smash the
front by the recognized Nazi methods. The Church's men
were able to meet these tactics, and also followed the good
maxim that attack is the best kind of defense. In their reply to the Department on behalf of the clergy and congregational councils, the bishops strongly condemned the
Department for trying to gain authority in the Church's
internal affairs, which was not permitted by law. The Department had in the second point in its circular of April
5th tried to give the clergy instructions by asking them
until further notice to emphasize the *purely eternal* and
constructive aspects of Gospel. The bishops declared that
this request had caused uncertainty regarding intentions,
and they defined the Church's right and duty in regard to
preaching in the following unambiguous words:

It is clear that it is the eternal Divine truths and above all the
salvation in Christ that are to be taught. But this teaching must
have the aim of recreating man's life on earth, from the innermost center of the heart to all regions where people live together. The eternal Word shall cast a light over daily affairs in
our own and everybody's lives. It is unavoidable in a sinful
world that there are things in the life of the individual as well
as the community that are condemned when put under the light
of the Word of God. If by "constructive" is meant "harmless"
it would constitute a denial of the God who wants to strike
home in the conscience, particularly when it is timely and hard-
to-take. Here it is necessary, of course, that God's Word treats
us all alike, without national, political or social distinction.

It is impossible to draw a line around God's Word and teaching, and to say that what is outside that line is the free domain
of the world. When certain people of the last generation pro-

claimed "Art for Art's sake" and wanted to *live* accordingly and as if morals were of no importance, the Church protested energetically and fought a bitter contest. This will always be the case, whether it be the artistic, political or economic fields that are concerned, where people act irresponsibly without considering whether their acts are in contradiction to the Word of God. Such a division of zones runs contrary to God's demand for the whole person and for the all-embracing of the common life of man. The call to Christ's disciples is still to be the light of the *world* and the salt of the *world.*

For all this the Church stands united in its confession and its common faith. Therefore each minister, upon ordination, has been entrusted with the holy duties of priesthood with "*right and authority*" to preach God's Word, to administer the holy sacraments, to care for the sick and the poor and the helpless, to comfort the sorrowful, to guide those who have lost their way, and *to do all that follows from his holy calling, in accordance with God's Word and the arrangement of our Church.*

These are the words of the service-book, and they are the law of the Norwegian Church. The Church has its regulations which can not be deviated from without weakening the Church's nature and the freedom of the Word. Among these regulations is also that of guarding the Word and Sacraments, which falls to the Church, alone, by its ordained and bound overseers. The congregational councils and the clergy therefore quite rightly assume that the bishops are the overseers of the Church, and that they will give guidance on matters of preaching and spiritual comfort and personal Christian life. The relationship which is laid down between bishops and pastors and congregation councils at the ordination is an expression of the sovereign authority of the Church in all that the confession describes as *the most innermost holy affairs.* This is the only possible foundation on which the Evangelical Lutheran Church can have a relationship with the State, which, on behalf of the people, arranges with the *outer affairs* of the people's Church.

The Church does not meddle in politics. From the Church's

point of view there is full freedom to choose forms of government and political arrangements so long as they do not violate the sacred right of each man as laid down in the Gospel. According to God, the Church exists in order to see that *every* order shall give freedom to life's salt as given us by God, and whereupon all human life shall be tested.

The invitation to concern itself purely with the hereafter and to leave the present in the good hands of the Nazis, could not have been rejected more plainly by the Church. A defeatist or less vigorous Church might easily have fallen for the temptation to withdraw from the unpleasant realities of life and to disappear into the distant world of theological edification. It would have suited the Nazi pagans very well to have directed Christ's Church into Heaven, *until further notice,* while they busily arranged things on earth in the style of the New Order. The Norwegian Church, however, replied by taking its stand in the center of the community with the right and duty to draw all fields of worldly activity, including politics, into the light and judgment of God's Word. In other words, the Church could not promise the quisling rulers that they would practice political neutrality in questions where the conscience was in any way concerned. The bishops emphasized, even more strongly than in the Pastoral Letter, the sovereign authority of the Church in the innermost holy affairs according to the law of the Norwegian Church. Instead of accepting the invitation of disappearing in the sky, the Church chose rather to take the risk of being driven into the earth and becoming a martyr Church.

A Smashing Indictment of the Quisling Regime

The Church also demonstrated its solidarity with the Norwegian people by participating in the sensational mass-protest of May 15, 1941, by forty-three national labor and professional organizations representing all sections of the Norwegian people. The protest, in the form of a letter addressed to Reichskommissar Terboven, was directed at the Nazi methods which had gradually been introduced in Norway. This protest had the same strong characteristics as the bishops' Pastoral Letter. Nothing indefinite or inconsequential was included.

It was complained here that the Nazi ministers had issued a number of decrees and made decisions which openly contravened international law, Norwegian law, and the ordinary Norwegian sense of justice. Mention was made of the fact that state and municipal servants were coerced into joining Nasjonal Samling with threats of dismissal if they did not do so, despite the assurance that nobody would be forced to join the party against his will. The document charged loyal and conscientious civil servants had been dismissed or suspended because they were not in good standing with the Nazis, and that membership of Nasjonal Samling had become prerequisite for appointment or promotion, while professional qualifications took second place. The protest finally pointed out that the unrest and irritation which these conditions had provoked among all classes of the people, were approaching the point of exasperation. Among the signers to this protest was Pastor L. Koren, representing the Norwegian Church's Association of Clergy.

This smashing condemnation of the Quisling rule from practically the whole of the Norwegian people aroused the ire of Nasjonal Samling, and its principal newspaper *Fritt Folk* was full of threats against the people who had signed the protest, especially those employed by the State or by local governmental authorities. In making these threats, Najonal Samling reckoned with the full support of the Germans, and quite naturally, because all the decrees concerned had obviously been issued at the initiative of the Reichskommissar. Terboven agreed to satisfy his lackeys by arranging a meeting in the chamber of the Norwegian parliament where the people concerned with the protest had to listen to a long harangue from the Reichskommissar typical of the new German "culture." They were told that their organizations had been taken over by the Nazis and would be run by *Treuhänder*. The proceedings came to an end when some of the leading men present were arrested by the Gestapo and taken to prison.

The Association of Clergy was allotted Feyling as its Nazi kommissar, and the consequences were that all members of the committee resigned their offices.

CHAPTER IV

THE NASJONAL SAMLING COMPLAINS OF RELIGIOUS ISOLATION

RELIABLE SOURCES RECKON that 30,000 Norwegians are members of Nasjonal Samling out of a total population of almost three million. This one per cent of the Norwegian population is far from representing an intellectual *elite*. Some of them are youths and misguided individuals who have been impressed by Nazi catch-phrases and dazzled by smart uniforms. Many are failures and ne'er-do-wells who had found it difficult to assert themselves in the free Norway, and who have found a natural field for their ambitions in Quisling's party. There are also quite a number of opportunists who reckoned with a certain German victory and who considered it wisest to book a seat early in the new Grosse Germania.

In order to tempt job-seekers and in order to force civil servants into the party, an order was issued in February, 1941, to the effect that every appointment in the public service—without regard to kind, pay, duration—had to be approved beforehand by Nasjonal Samling's Personnel Office for Public Offices. It was also decided that every announcement of a vacancy should include the clause: "Applicants must give details about earlier and present political party affiliations." These regulations also applied to appointments in the State Church. But despite all such tactics, despite the progress made in Norway and elsewhere by the German forces in the first year of the occupation, and despite the complete control by the Nazis of the Norwegian press and radio (even the parish magazines were censored in order to insure that they were not used "as means of spreading unrest"), the ranks of the quislings remained just as thin.

There were never many active Christians among the Nazis. Only a handful of ministers, 27 out of the 1000 in Norway, were active quislings. The percentage of quislings among the church-goers was as a rule even smaller. Their position soon became unenviable, even though they were supported by the full power of the government, as well as by German bayonets. The quisling ministers lost all contact with their congregations. Church attendances fell to a minimum wherever they tried to preach. Pastor Sigmund Feyling faced a congregation of thirteen when he gave his farewell sermon in Egersund before leaving the town to take up a new appointment as secretary for the Department of Church and Education. Another prominent Nazi cleric, Pastor Blessing Dahle of Ullern, also lost practically his entire following, and was given a long "leave" in order to "prepare for the work of aligning the Church to the New Order." Things came to such a desperate pass that a correspondent declared in *Fritt Folk,* probably with considerable justification, that the Nasjonal Samling ministers were among those who suffered most, and he urged all members of Nasjonal Samling to attend church regularly when NS pastors were preaching.

Ostracism was one of the few weapons which the Nazis could not take away from the Norwegian people, and it was a weapon of very considerable force. Nothing can better show the solidarity of the people against the oppressors and traitors than the recurring complaints from the Nazis about coldness shown them and the loneliness they felt. Such complaints were given official expression as early as March, 1941, when Norway's "Tiny Goebbels," Gulbrand Lunde, complained in a speech in Bergen about the "terrific spiritual terrorism" to which Nasjonal Samling was subjected. At about the same time a special group of Christians was formed within Nasjonal Samling in Skien. This group received the name of "Kristen Samling" (Christian Union) despite the fact that a *real* Christian union had been formed outside Nasjonal Samling long ago. This was indirectly admitted by the Nazis themselves when they wrote in *Fritt Folk* that recent events had to be interpreted as a union of the entire Christian population of Norway against Nasjonal Samling. It was explained officially that a special Christian group had to be formed within Nasjonal Samling because "we Christians who have joined Nasjonal Samling are no longer welcome within the communities of faith we previously belonged to." They openly complained that they felt themselves "frozen out."

In the above-mentioned circular of April 5th from the Department of Church and Education to pastors and congregational councils it was also asked how it could possibly occur that members of the congregation were "frozen out" from Holy Communion and the church services (for political reasons), and it was suggested that the congregational councils should investigate the matter. The Department warned that there might be "incalculable consequences for the freedom of the Church and Christian work." The bishops replied that no one had expressed any uneasiness to them about such a "freezing out," and that the Department had not submitted any complaints to them nor asked them to deal with this regrettable state of affairs.

The bishops admitted that such regrettable divisions of the people were to be found in personal relationships, and that these would also characterize human associations. But they said the congregational councils, as such, had no power to smooth out the difficulties which such divisions might produce. Nor could the clergy interfere in the internal affairs of voluntary organizations, declared the bishops, except in a purely advisory capacity when the opportunity arose. It appeared, on the whole, impossible to give any instructions with universal application, except that one should always be the servant of love even when there were *human contradictions which could not, or should not, be concealed or veiled.*

One of the men who had been "frozen out" was Arne Rydland, who had been a district secretary for the Home Mission. In May, 1941, he began to publish a new journal, *Christian Union,* with the support and blessing of the Department of Church and Education. The object of the journal was to form a link between all members of Nasjonal Samling who were religiously interested. Whether it succeeded in melting the ice and dispelling the loneliness felt by the members is not known.

Nasjonal Samling speech-makers and writers, however, are still harping with great bitterness on this "isolation." Finn Halvorsen, one of the Nazi leaders of culture, in a book-review in the *Aftenposten* of June 12, 1941, strongly attacked the people who call themselves Christians but who "cling to hate while preaching God's Word," and he calls on the Church to recognize its hour of destiny:

If the men of the Church during this new era show cold passivity towards the change, or, what is worse, show an unfriendly attitude towards our ruling party and our form of government, or even openly sympathize with that country whose goal it is to smash National Socialism and the authoritarian form of government, then the Church may risk missing the bus. When the men of the Church eventually discover that they have backed the wrong horse, that the authoritarian rule is to be a permanent rule which the Church must reckon with in the future, and therefore wish to commence to cooperate with the State, then it *might* be that the opportunity is no longer there and will never return.

These lines are quoted because they exemplify some of the most prominent characteristics of quisling propaganda for the New Order in Norway: cynical opportunism and contempt for moral values. Even Halvorsen, who should be one of the leading lights of Norwegian Nazi culture, reduces the Church struggle, on which depends the foundation of Norwegian culture for generations, to a mere bet, to a question of backing the right horse, or a question of catching the last bus before it is too late. Against this low-browed opportunism the Norwegian Church stands out radiant.

Another quisling leader of culture, the author Kristen Gundelach, proposed in October, 1941, that assistant pastors should be appointed in every parish to meet the religious needs of Nasjonal Samling's members. After mentioning "the black-listing of people who listen to positively adjusted pastors," Gundelach declared that something must be done as soon as possible "to permit members of the ruling party, wherever they may live, to go to church and listen to services without feeling that they are condemned in the eyes of others, and to be married, to have their children christened and their dead buried without the assistance of a pastor who secretly supports the enemy." He proposed that a sufficient number of assistant pastors be appointed to hold services in the parish churches once, twice, or more times a month, according to the number of Nasjonal Samling members in the congregation. It must also become the duty of Nasjonal Samling members, he said, to attend church every Sunday when a Nasjonal Samling pastor was preaching. Then, Gundelach rejoiced, they would subsequently be able to demand more and more Sundays and gradually oust the old pastors from their churches!

This proposal is probably more a reflection of a certain mental attitude than a practical plan; and it undeniably looks better on paper than in practice. Even if members of Nasjonal Samling were expressly summoned to attend church, it would still be extremely difficult to marshal a majority in Norwegian congregations from the miserable one or two per cent of the Norwegian people who are quislings. The other great difficulty would be to supply a sufficiently large number of assistant pastors with the necessary faith in the "leader" and Nasjonal Samling. There are not many in Norway.

Ragnar Skancke, Minister of Church and Education, spoke rather optimistically on this point on September 25, 1941, the anniversary of the day when Nasjonal Samling came to power. He declared that "the number of pastors who say 'yes' to the New Order is constantly increasing; the majority of pastors recently appointed can be guaranteed as understanding the New Era in which we live and are willing to work for positive co-operation between State and Church." He revealed that all theological students were being asked about their political beliefs and that they were not to be given an appointment unless they displayed a friendly attitude. Skancke did not supply any figures with which to support his claims.

CHAPTER V

THE HIRD AND THE EDUCATION OF
THE YOUNG

NAZISM, LIKE CHRISTIANITY, demands the whole of an individual. Thus it reveals itself as being not simply an ordinary political movement, but also a religion. An *ersatz-religion,* true enough, which in spite of all its nihilistic lack of principle has a firm core in its heathen power worship. Nasjonal Samling has a reassuring clause in its program to the effect that Christian principles shall be protected. Many simple-hearted people have at various times been enticed by this clause, which is used wherever it may serve to pacify anxious Christians or win their support. The acid test of the promise is found in its application in relation to the rising generation.

In Germany the Nazis have, on the whole, succeeded in infecting the youth with heathen principles, while Christian instruction has suffered correspondingly. What is the situation in occupied Norway? In this sphere, too, there have been the usual attempts to make a faithful copy of the German original. These attempts at making a *Hitlerjugend* of Norwegian youth have so far had little success, not because of any lack of zeal on the part of Norwegian Nazis, but because the Church and the whole of the Norwegian people have stood on guard, and because the patriotism of Norwegian youth has been too strong for the Nazi poison.

The bishops had already sounded the alarm in their Pastoral Letter, when they pointed at the attacks made by the Hird and at the spirit of force which was being aroused among young people. The Hird contains what in Nazi eyes are ideal specimens of Norwegian youth, the vanguard and first sons of the New Order. The education of the members of the Hird must therefore be considered as a model for the education and ideals of the all future Norwegian youth, if that Nazi nightmare, Grosse Germania, should become a reality. It is the straw that shows which way the wind is blowing. It is, therefore, of interest to see what sort of ideals the Hird flaunts, and to what degree the principles of Christianity are protected within the Hird's rank.

Orvar Saether, former Chief of Staff for the Hird, was for a long time entrusted with the ideological leadership of the Hird, and has also been the editor of *Hirdmannen,* a supplement to *Fritt Folk.* At a Hird rally at Larvik in April, 1941, he stated that Nasjonal Samling builds on a triple foundation: (1) Race; (2) the Nordic view of life; and (3) National Socialism. He sought to arouse racial pride among his uncritical young audience with statements such as that all great cultures were created by the Germanic race; that of all the people in the world the Norwegians were those who had the purest Germanic blood and were therefore presumably the most talented; that "against us stand the Jews who want to destroy us, and if we do not win the present war it will be the end of the Germanic race." Orvar Saether also declared that Norwegians must create a new Germanic ideology which they would find by reading of how their forefathers had lived.

In a speech at a Hird jamboree at the Colosseum in Oslo on November 2nd of the same year, Saether developed his theme. He switched from ancient Nordic mythology to the present day, completely ignoring the nine hundred years of Christianity in Norway from the time of Stiklestad to April 9, 1940, when Norway was invaded. Perhaps this period was too "contaminated" by the Nazarene religion from the non-Germanic Palestine.

An essential feature of Germanic philosophy (said Saether), is the belief in the existence of two universal principles. They are Odin's principle, which can also be called the Germanic blood principle or the good principle; and Loki's principle, which can also be called the Jewish blood principle or the evil principle. It is Germanic blood against Jewish blood. The ancients also held the view that it was not predetermined which of the two races should be triumphant in the world. Fate would not aid either side. The races themselves would decide, and they would decide in battle. And the issue would show who would triumph, but it was the duty of every good German to serve the good and not the evil. Ragnarok is the last great battle between the Jewish and the Nordic blood. Many hold the opinion that it is Ragnarok we are experiencing today. And with sacrifice and faithfulness and with sword in hand we must see that the Jews lose and that we win.

Vidkun Quisling's Hirdmen shall win this battle. The good must triumph. The Germanic blood must get the opportunity to build the new world which will stretch from the Urals in the East to the Atlantic in the West, from the Arctic Sea in the North to the burning sun in the South.

Germanism is the belief in the triumph of the Germanic blood in Europe. Germanism is belief in the good.

Against us stand the Jews and their kingdom; and by German blood it must be regarded as hell.

Hirdmen, we will follow our leader's vision! We will create a true and good Germanism.

The third great pillar in our new society is something really new, and something which has not been seen since the time of Odin. It is that the Norwegian and Germanic soils are now serving one great purpose: that of the New Europe.

This Old Norse "blood religion" or "blood soup" which the new youth is to live on, is made from the well-known pagan recipe of Nazi Germany. It bears all the signs of having been brewed by cynical power politicians without real religious belief (apart from the belief in power), who have found it expedient to back up their schemes with the fanatic strength which such an ersatz-religion can induce. The Nazis, therefore, do not find it beyond them to speak on this subject with two or more tongues. Besides handing out this new-pagan Germanic blood-and-race religion to their own advance guards, they are also quite able to pose before another public as crusaders and defenders of Christian values. All that matters is that by such trickery they may be able to gain an immediate reinforcement of strength. Naïve and simple-minded Christians and perverted Nazi pastors are needed just as much as the young Germanic heathen who are prepared to die for their faith in Hitler and Quisling. If it serves their purpose, the Nazi leaders are quite prepared to allow their Germanic Hirdmen to attend Church service. They are, in short, politically and religiously omnivorous, so long as their victims are willing to co-operate and permit themselves to be digested and utilized by their masters.

Not only the above-mentioned speeches, but also a whole multitude of other facts show that the new-paganism is an important factor in the nazification of Norwegian youth. *Hirdmannen,* the special Hird journal, has a whole array of vikings on its "mast-head," and is always moving in the same mythological, pre-Christian spheres. It has printed an entire catechism of the old mythology in the form of "Questions for Hirdmen." Here are two questions and answers quoted from *Hirdmannen* for February 8, 1941:

Q. Is it necessary for us today to know the old Germanic history?
A. Yes, one must know the foundations for one's people's way of thinking.
Q. What does such a knowledge bind one to do?
A. To live boldly, gallantly, and loyally.

On May 3, 1941, *Hirdmannen* wrote that "Nordic mythology brings us to the heart of a religion which is in fuller agreement with the eternal values than a religion which came from outside. . . . People who have honour, faith and honesty do not need a God from whom to beg forgiveness."

The same organ for the Hird wrote on January 1, 1941: "There is an unbroken line from the heathen blood-sacrifices to our present-day Christmas festival." The Christmas festival is therefore no longer to be Christian, but "the great mid-winter festival."

The pagan tendencies of the Norwegian people were

fully discussed in an article in *Fritt Folk* on October 11, 1941, under the title "The Education of Boys in the Northern Viking Period." The article pointed out that it was characteristic of the heathen Norwegian community that all Norwegian talent, physical as well as spiritual, art and fighting ability, could be traced back to the God of war. The article also pointed out that in the Viking period disputes were settled by battle, so that the strongest held the right, and that the ordinary man did not think twice if he could gain an advantage, large or small, by sacrificing another man. Everyone lived in suspense:

The glorious example of their forefathers, enhanced by saga and song, was always in the thoughts of the men and filled them with an indomitable urge to do great deeds, and with a ruthless aspiration to fame. The great deeds they aspired to were deeds of war, which would be to the honor of their family and enhance their own position after death.

In agreement with the moral views of that time, which were concerned least of all with humanistic considerations, we find at the beginning of our recorded history that our forefathers were Vikings and merchants. Peaceful occupations such as farming and fishing were regarded as essential sources of food, as well as a means of founding a fortune, and many cattle were a good backing, but caring for a herd did not give prestige, so that this work was delegated to inferior men and slaves. The free-born youth sallied forth, far out over land and sea. They had to go forth if they were to win fame and wealth.

It is not difficult to see how this ancient Viking spirit is diametrically opposed to all Christian ideals, and how it breaks up the entire Christian foundations of society. The "leader" himself, Vidkun Quisling, also likes to swathe his speeches in ancient Nordic mysticism. In his speech on Midsummer Day in June, 1941, he said:

We need these old symbols which remind us of so much, and we have resurrected these symbols in our red and golden banner which waves over the Nasjonal Samling movement. We do not want to return to paganism, but we do want to return to the courage to live which that period gave our people. We will be like the bird which crowns our emblem, and which is not afraid to look into the rays of the sun. These are the thoughts with which we want again to inspire our people, so that they can stand armed in the battle which now rages within us and around us. Because Ragnarok has now come.

Here Quisling himself has identified Nasjonal Samling symbols with the old heathen symbols and has accepted the "courage to live" of the Viking period, although with appropriate Nazi duplicity he has denied that he wanted to return to paganism. The "crusade" against the Soviet Union had then just begun. His new secretary in the Department of Church and Education, Pastor Sigmund Feyling, had also just issued a Christian booklet to be used for religious instruction in the schools, which had the Nasjonal Samling sun-cross symbol on the cover.

Together with this Germanic paganism the Nazis have coupled a determined propaganda, aimed at defying Quisling in the best Hitlerian style. It is emphasized that Quisling has an old Norwegian genealogy, and it has *almost* been said that it goes back to Odin himself! He is described in the Nazi press as "the trusted agent of Providence," as "the man with the prophetic eye" who foresaw all the present events, a man with supernatural powers. Thus, in its homage to Quisling on the anniversary of the German attack on Norway, *Fritt Folk* wrote:

Above the gigantic, unique picture of April 9th arise two giant figures; Adolf Hitler and Vidkun Quisling, the great Germanic leaders. Unostentatious and simple like natural forces, but also huge and irresistible.

And in another column *Fritt Folk* declared:

Norway's leader can laugh as the young Germanic gods laugh when they lavish eternal gifts on grateful and ungrateful, righteous and unrighteous.

When Quisling appears at meetings, he is met with fanfares and his supporters reverently accord him all the ritual of idolatry. One can imagine the feelings of ordinary Norwegians when they see and hear Quisling described as "God's gift to the Norwegian people" and "the man who was sent by God to save Norway."

Whether it is mental weakness or simply cold political speculation which has encouraged Quisling to seek a personal place among the Germanic gods, shall remain unsaid. At all events he fully appreciates the value of ensconcing his treacherous policy in youthful minds with some form of religious fanaticism. This found expression in a speech to young people in Oslo on February 1, 1941, when he expressly emphasized that the Norwegian youth's belief in the common political aims of Germany and Norway must become so strong that it assumes "a downright religious character."

In November, 1941, *Fritt Folk* published a report on the burial of a little Hirdboy who had been killed in an accident. The article placed Quisling on a level with Our Lord Himself:

> There is one bond which binds us together more strongly than the feelings of family or kin,—the belief in Nasjonal Samling and our leader Quisling . . .
>
> May you who stand outside the ranks of the Hird understand what a gift we possess in our faith in God and in our Leader. We hope the majority of our people may receive this gift.

It is easy to believe the reports which say that some of Nasjonal Samling's most cold-blooded propagandists have privately admitted that they were attempting to repeat the "success" which was achieved in Germany in presenting Hitler as a supernatural being. They should have added that when such a propaganda campaign reaches its successful conclusion, nothing would then prevent Quisling from following Hitler's example of attacking the Church with all the forces at his command.

The fruits of training in the heathen principles of racial superiority, arrogance, and power-lust soon showed themselves in the above-mentioned attacks by the Hird when those misguided, uniformed bands of young people—often of very low intelligence—began to put their theories into practice. But the conditions in Norway were not so favorable for brutal lawlessness as they had been in Germany. There was the resistance not only of the Church but also of a united people. And that resistance was often of a robust nature, so that the Hirdboys were sometimes given some of their own medicine. The result was that the Hird, owing to its few members, had to conduct itself with greater care, and Nazi propaganda even tried for a while to portray its members as models of good discipline, politeness, and helpfulness. Some impression of the spirit with which these quisling storm-troopers are infected is given by this statement made by Hird Adjutant Aall to the magazine *Varden* in Skien:

The Hird includes the elite of the Nasjonal Samling movement. It is above the police and nearly above the law. Even if the Hird is above the law, the individual Hirdman is not above the law. It is only when a leader or a Hirdman acts as a representative of the local Hird, and orders or demands something on its behalf, that all other interests must stand aside. The Hird is not responsible to the police. The Hird-leaders are only responsible to their superior officers—the General Staff in Oslo and Quisling himself. The Hird's aim is to live in accordance with those ideals which the Nasjonal Samling movement champions.

In its capacity as the chosen medium of Nazi lawlessness, the Hird was naturally enough soon employed in actions against the Jews. There had never been any Jewish problem in Norway. The Jews in Norway had been few in number and their conduct above reproach, but Quisling tried to create a Jewish problem by propaganda, and he initiated a general campaign of persecution against the Jews. In a six-column article he called for vengeance against the Jews. The Hird was instructed to strike at Jewish shops, and it was not long before they began to smash windows or befoul them with anti-Semitic inscriptions. The public was urged to boycott Jewish shops, but the Norwegians immediately reacted against this Nazi form of racial persecution by patronizing these shops more frequently than ever before. Dean Fjellbu publicly

protested at the reign of terror against the Jews in Trondheim, as well as against the treatment of the hostages from
Lofoten, and was heavily fined for it.

"The New Youth is being trained without hindrance
from democracy, with faith in its leader, its movement,
and the future of its country," said a speaker on the Oslo
radio. But that does not prevent it from honoring the
Church with its attendance at an occasional Hird-rally,
especially when an NS pastor, who understands the New
Order, is available. There was, for instance, a special service for Nasjonal Samling youth in Our Saviour's Church
in Oslo on September 29, 1941, with Pastor Andreas
Gjerdi in the pulpit. The Nazis formed a garland of flags
round the altar, and the pastor spoke about Norwegian national and moral decadence before the 9th of April awak-
ened the people. He also spoke of war against godless
Bolshevism and "for the ideas and ideals which our leader
has held before us."

A visit by the Hird to Garmo church in the Gulbrands-
dal in May, 1941, had a sequel in the press which is rather
revealing. The thirty Hird-youths were very disappointed
because the pastor had not taken sufficient notice of their
presence in God's House. Ansgar Brekke, a Nasjonal
Samling "press-leader," gave expression to this disappoint-
ment in an article in *Gudbrandsdölen* where he admon-
ished the pastor as follows:

The pastor did not have a single word or glance for us Hirdmen. There would have been no difficulty in taking another
half-hour for offering some words on the Hird-detachment, as
he could not have been unaware of its presence. If he had the

slightest appreciation of his serious calling he would have felt himself both religiously and nationally obliged to do so.

We had done this man the honor of sitting beneath his pulpit. My Hird-comrades and I are not tempted to do so again.

The work of nazifying the youth outside the little circle of quislings had gone very slowly. Before the last crisis in Church and school, beginning February 1, 1942, certain attacks had been launched against the schools, but on the whole such moves had been repelled. The teaching profession resisted the attempts at making the schools politically uniform, and the plan of introducing special propaganda hours for Nasjonal Samling in the schools was doomed to failure without the co-operation of the teachers. The order that portraits of Quisling were to be hung up in all classrooms met such a wall of resistance that it had to be repealed. Forced school visits to Nazi propaganda exhibitions, such as the *Hitlerjugend* exhibition, were turned into complete farces and even produced spontaneous anti-Nazi demonstrations by the children. In Oslo the youngsters went off to the Palace square and sang the national anthem and other patriotic songs. Interference by the Hird in the work of the schools inspired school strikes at several places. The Nazi authorities found it necessary to threaten to establish their own schools where Norwegian patriots could be brought and forcibly fed with Nazism.

The Nazi authorities have also been handicapped by the fact that they lack both personnel and textbooks suitable for the New Order. In the field of religious instruction Feyling had made a start by issuing a new textbook. This book aroused wide interest by the explanation which its author had attached to the Fourth Commandment. In this connection he had been able to smuggle in the name of the "leader" in the following way:

If Norway is to become a good home, everyone must feel his responsibility. Consideration for the people must precede all other considerations. Public interest must precede private interest. Before all else we owe allegiance to the leader and the government. To oppose the State's authority would be to oppose God's order and is punishable.

This book was approved by Minister Skancke and his sister-in-law and official adviser, Kari Aas, but the bishops told the congregational councils that they did not approve of the book being used in the schools. The book was not used.

The series of articles by Fredrik Ramm in *Morgenbladet* must be regarded as a positive counter-weight to the pagan Germanic poison propaganda. In his survey of Norwegian literature down through the ages he emphasized the Christian influence and the Christian values in the Norwegian cultural heritage. Editor Ramm, who is a well-known worker in the Oxford Group Movement, was arrested for the second time during the state of emergency in September, 1941, and was sentenced to life imprisonment.

CHAPTER VI

THE CHURCH AND HITLER'S "CRUSADE"

IT IS NO secret that Bishop Berggrav's rôle as the foremost leader of the Church worried and irritated the Germans, and that they therefore at an early stage of the struggle already had the intention of arresting him. Wikborg, a lawyer in Oslo, who had acted as an intermediary between the patriotic clergy and the German authorities, was asked by the Germans what the consequences would be if Bishop Berggrav were arrested. The lawyer replied that there would not be a bishop in Norway the next day. The Germans suggested that one of the deans might take Berggrav's place. The lawyer replied that no bishop would consecrate a dean who would take over Berggrav's position after the latter's arrest. The Germans developed their theme and said it would be possible to call in a Swedish bishop for the consecration of Berggrav's successor. Wikborg replied that such a possibility could only exist in the Germans' own wishful fancies.

The Nazis then abandoned their idea of disposing of Berggrav by direct arrest. The inquiry may only have been a warning shot. But they certainly entertained hopes of gaining their ends by the more indirect means of getting a foothold within the Episcopal Senate for one of their own men. One of their clerical tools had for a long

YOU ARE INVITED to a HARVEST
Time Social

Given by—the young people Commun-
Baptist Church

PLACE— 4186 Park Ave. The 13x.

DATE— Nov. 1, 1947

Time— 7:30

Dress Informal

RSVP not later than Oct. 25 to
Miss Mary Javier
1895 Belmont Ave.

time been openly seeking a more exalted position within
the Church and would most certainly be willing to help.
By a new decree Reichskommissar Terboven ordered that
the age-limit for public servants should be reduced from
70 to 65 years. This gave the Nazi authorities an opportunity to dismiss two of the bishops, Stören and Maroni.
This was done, and six pastors were also dismissed. All
these men, except two, had been members of the council
of the Norwegian Association of Clergy, so the aim of the
new decree was plain enough. The dismissals caused a
great sensation and much unrest in Church circles, and
Bishop Berggrav protested so energetically to the German
authorities that Terboven annulled the dismissals. This
was undoubtedly a great blow for Nasjonal Samling. If
they had succeeded in getting one of their own men into
the Episcopal Senate, they would have been able to dismiss the others without breaking the apostolic succession
and would have given the nazification of the Church some
semblance of legality.

The reason Terboven on this occasion took care to avoid
any open, bitter quarrel with the Church was presumably
that Hitler was at that time about to launch his "crusade"
against the Soviet Union and had instructed his servants to
treat the Church carefully and to try to initiate active co-
operation with it against the godless Bolsheviks. The Germans attacked Russia on June 22nd, and the "crusade"
was started with much publicity and speech-making. A
so-called "Norwegian Legion" was formed, and the earlier
Norwegian sympathy for Finland was exploited to the
full in the campaign to enroll recruits. Altogether it was

an ambitious scheme to mix the cards and to encourage the Norwegian people to forget the war against their own oppressors and thus entice them to fight for Hitler against the Russians. It was intended that the Church should play a very important part in this grandiose scheme of deception.

However, Hitler had once more underrated the Norwegian people's political intelligence and their ability to think for themselves. Propaganda for the "Norwegian Legion" became a fiasco. Norwegian youth refused to follow the Swastika into Russia, except for a few quislings who more, or often less, willingly donned the German uniform. And the Church was silent. Gulbrand Lunde, Norway's "Little Göbbels," asked impatiently in a speech: "Where does the Church stand today in this matter?" Eventually, after a month's time, a tiny squeak was heard in the form of a "Call to the Norwegian People" signed in all by the twenty-seven quislings among the Norwegian clergy. The text was as follows:

The final, decisive battle against Bolshevism and the international godlessness movement is now in progress. Everyone must realize now what is at stake. On it depends whether our children shall continue to have a Christian upbringing and a Christian school. On it depends how far we shall continue to retain the Christian faith, morality and culture in this land.

The undersigned pastors call on the Norwegian people to stand together during this fateful period for our land and people.

For Norway and Finland against Bolshevism.

The support which this proclamation received was certainly not impressive. It lacked, especially, the support of higher Church officials and leaders, which would be necessary if it were to carry any kind of weight or significance. The proclamation was issued to coincide with an episcopal meeting which all Norway's bishops were holding in Oslo. And the bishops were not left in any doubt as to what the Nazi authorities expected them to do. *Fritt Folk* wrote:

The Norwegian people have been thinking for a long time that our Churchmen should speak out. And it is a pleasure to see that as soon as the battle began the Norwegian pastors sent out a call to the Norwegian people urging them to rise up in the fight against Bolshevism. At an episcopal meeting which is now being held the Norwegian Clergy will make a declaration which the Norwegian people have long been waiting for.

On the same day Olga Bjoner, Quisling's "woman-peasant leader," tried to arouse the proper crusading spirit in the Norwegian women by broadcasting on the Bolshevik godlessness and the danger for Christianity and home.

The episcopal meeting ended without any declaration being issued about the "crusade," and *Fritt Folk* wrote bitterly on July 25th:

We felt quite sure, *despite all,* that the episcopal meeting could not be held *now* without naturally the main theme for discussion being the fight against the mortal enemy of Christianity—and it is a mortal enemy who has been openly recognized and pointed out by the Church itself during 23 years. But we were greatly mistaken. In a letter to *Fritt Folk* Bishop Berggrav writes:
"The war-political question which you discuss in your article, has not been made an issue at the episcopal meeting and naturally was not among the matters discussed."

A warm and earnest word of good sense from that quarter could have been of use, quite undoubtedly. Therefore it did not come.

This rejection was so brief and to the point that it acted virtually as a blow on the nose and greatly enraged the quislings' principal newspaper. It did not tend to allay this rage that the same meeting had refused to authorize the use of Feyling's Nazi book of Christian instruction in the schools. Nor that the meeting had sent a Pastoral Letter to pastors and congregations to the effect that they had persuaded the occupation authorities to "move with lenience." The bishops had personally got in touch with Terboven and warned him about the developments in Norway. They had advised that the occupation authorities act with care, and that the administration respect Norwegian law and custom. The bishops had then received assurance that the occupation authorities had no cause to act harshly and that "lenience" would be shown.

Nasjonal Samling felt that it had suffered another humiliation similar to that resulting from the forty-three organizations' protest which was made directly to the Reichskommissar. This time Terboven had listened in a spirit of conciliation and in his promises to the bishops had acted over the heads of the quisling administration; this made the matter twice as bitter for Nasjonal Samling. *Fritt Folk,* therefore, concluded its article with a warning that lenience was no longer appropriate, but dangerous and unnecessary, towards people who systematically used their well-paid State posts and their consequent authority to undermine Norway's future in the New Europe. The time had come, said the paper, for these men to suffer the consequences of their contentions.

The refusal of the bishops to support Hitler's "crusade" against Bolshevism was made the signal for a tremendous campaign in the Nazi press against the Church in general and Bishop Berggrav in particular. *Hirdmannen* wrote that "those clerics who do not do the natural duty of every Christian by supporting the fight for the existence of Christianity, they are not Christians, but hypocrites who misuse the Christian name and the ministry for the sake of the salary." The journal threatened that these pastors would not be forgotten after the world settlement had been made. In an open letter they were accused of being "spiritual saboteurs."

Bishop Berggrav became the target of a series of "open letter" attacks which then followed. Typical of the "serious questions" thus posed for the bishop is this one: "Are you afraid of your colleague, the Archbishop of Canterbury, who, according to the London Radio, prays to God for the victory of the Bolshevik associates?" Or a request such as this: "Cast away the mask! Show us London's face from the altar. Let the Internationale roar from the organ in Our Saviour's Church, so that one could believe the Devil himself was the organist." *Fritt Folk* published a letter of thanks which it was said had been sent by the bishops in the Ukraine to Hitler, and left the adjoining column blank with the words: "This space is reserved for Bishop Berggrav's reply." The bishop remained silent and the paper then printed a picture of a Nazi procession where a banner was carried with the following inscription in huge letters:

"Do *you* defend murder against women and children, Bishop Berggrav?" Under the picture was an open space with the words: "Here the bishop can still reply, but now he must hurry a bit. It costs 75 crowns a day at the present advertising rates to keep this space open." The time went by, and the Nazi Press began to write about Bishop Berggrav's "inciting and demonstrative silence" which must imply, the papers declared, that he had placed himself "on the side of the Archbishop of Canterbury and the Red church workers."

Despite all their failures the Nasjonal Samling authorities had still not given up the hope of inducing some of the clergy to support the Nazi proclamation. This was made clear by a circular which the Department of Church and Education sent to all the country's pastors under the date of September 11, 1941. A copy of an "Appeal to the Norwegian People" was enclosed, with requests that it be approved and returned, duly signed. Those who found themselves unable to approve the proclamation were asked to give their reasons. Failure to reply would be regarded as disapproval of the proclamation, the Nazis warned. It was also stated in the circular that influential quarters had requested that the clergy should be given an opportunity to support the appeal, and that it had caused grave concern in wide circles when high dignitaries of the Church had declared that the current war against Bolshevism and the godlessness-movement was a "war-political question" which "naturally was not" among the questions discussed at a clerical meeting. This rather high-pressured request from the Department apparently did not succeed, either, because the Department did not deem it advisable to make public the results.

There is, on the other hand, another document of interest in this connection, namely a joint reply sent to the Department on September 19th by the clergy in West Telemark. It was declared here that the clergy could *not* give the appeal their approval or sign it. They declared it— "both in form, content and principle"—represented an unpermissible and dangerous mixture of religion and politics. It should also be remembered, said these pastors, that one was today in a position of compulsion, that the Norwegian people were at war, and that it appeared to them that the "Appeal to the Norwegian People" (with its call to rise against godlessness) would, under the present conditions, only serve to incite civil war. They, therefore, urgently requested the Department to recall the circular and halt the appeal.

The Nazis had difficulty in swallowing this humiliating collapse of their grand plans to drag the Church with them into the "crusade" against Bolshevism. Thus, in an article discussing Terboven's speech on the so-called "Harvest Thanksgiving Festival" in Oslo, *Fritt Folk* (October 12, 1941) threatened:

If the Church's bishops work on the assumption that the Church shall be a state within the State which freely and unhindered can choose its own political line, or that it can work against or co-operate with whom it likes, then these leaders have placed the seal on their own activities. They have, under the protection of the Church's freedom, defended their own Church-political positions instead of defending the basic values of Christianity. But by so doing they have placed themselves

outside, and the State organs alone can draw the ripe consequences of their deeds.

The atmosphere became so tense that the Church had to
be prepared for a crisis at any moment. But the Church
remained firm and unshakeable on its foundations, knowing full well that any compromise with Nazism would be
fatal. It knew what "co-operation" really meant. Nasjonal
Samling was demanding no more and no less than that the
clergy should support Nasjonal Samling's policy with the
authority of the Church and Christianity, and even of God.
Pastors and pulpit orators, according to the Nazi plan,
were to preach to the people that Quisling's party was an
instrument in the service of a higher power. A foretaste of
what was demanded was given on September 14th when
Sigmund Feyling broadcast a "Thanksgiving Day" sermon
based on the text of Christ's cure of the ten lepers, and
suggested that the present-day lepers were those who, in
the quisling language, suffered from "English sickness."
He asked his listeners whether they had thanked God for
sending the Germans to save them from this leprosy. He
also asked whether they had thanked God for sending
them Quisling, he who saw the treachery of the King and
Government, and who sacrificed his health for the well-
being of the Norwegian people. He finally asked his listeners whether they had thanked God for the fact that Norwegian boys were to be found who, moved by a spiritual
impulse, had even sacrificed their lives in order to save
their people from the Russian godlessness.

Such is Norwegian Christianity in the official Nazi
edition!

No wonder that the Church leaders found it necessary to keep very careful guard. Bishop Berggrav intervened immediately when the Department of Church and Education made a fresh attempt, as unlawful as it was unsuccessful, to interfere in the Church's internal affairs. Without consulting the Oslo bishop, the Department ordered the pastors to mention, during their services on Sunday, September 22nd, a "British crime" consisting of the recent sinking of the two Norwegian ships, *Richard With* and *Bardöy* off the Norwegian coast. Only a few quisling pastors complied with this order.

The Department replied to Bishop Berggrav's reprimand by sending a circular to all Norwegian pastors. It declared that the Oslo bishop had no special position among the bishops; that he was not the first among equals; and still less was he the Norwegian Church's primate. The time of popedom was long past in Norway, said the letter, and the Department was going to make sure that it was not brought back through the back door. The Department further declared that it had the right to use any bishops it liked as advisers. It maintained that according to the Church Law the bishops had no right to make decisions in conflict with the Department, and concluded by threatening to return to the question of limiting the bishops' administrative duties, which could only mean curtailment of the bishops' authority.

This was a gauntlet tossed at the Church leaders by Nasjonal Samling's administration, a challenge to a decisive test of strength for the power and authority in the Church.

CHAPTER VII

QUISLING'S RETURN TO POWER

THE FALTERING campaign to nazify Norway was given new life and vigor with the elevation, on February 1, 1942, of Vidkun Quisling to the office of "Minister-President" in the so-called "State Act at Akershus." Norway's arch-traitor was thereby put back in the position of government leadership which he had held immediately after the German invasion. At that time his leadership had lasted only a few days. How long would it now last?

It was obvious that Quisling had obtained his promotion on the basis of assurances made to his German overlords that he had a program which could and would bring the Norwegians into line. That program has never been made public, but the people did not have to wait long for indications of its nature. As Minister-President, Quisling soon began proclaiming laws of the most arbitrary and ruthless kind. One of the first stipulated that all children between the ages of 10 and 18 years were to be members of an organization called the *Ungdomsfylking,* Norwegian model of the notorious *Hitlerjugend* of Germany; the youngsters were to be required to "do service" (of a character never fully described) and were to be indoctrinated with Nazi principles.

More typical of the torrent of new laws that flowed

from Quisling was that which established a new national
organization for teachers, the *Laerersamband*; it provided
that all teachers were automatically members of this association and as such would be required to bring all their
teaching into harmony with the New Order. Other laws
set up similar national and nazified organizations for all
the lawyers in the country, all the shipowners, all the
publishers, and so on. Heralded but never proclaimed was
a law to unite all laborers in a vast Nazi union.

By these developments, almost all of which occurred
during February, Quisling's program became discernible.
It was, in brief, to forcefully reorganize the entire Norwegian society according to trades and professions, with
indication that in the future government of the nation the
old idea of geographical representation would be discarded
and the people would be represented instead by individuals
of their own calling. There was no assurance that these individuals would be designated by popular vote.

Whatever Quisling's program was, it held no attraction
for the people of Norway. If Quisling had hoped to catch
the public off its guard, he was gravely disappointed. Nobody was napping, least of all the Church of Norway. The
Church immediately sensed the full import of Quisling's
promotion, and Church leaders did not wait to be directly
attacked by new decrees before launching a counter-
offensive which soon had the Quisling program hopelessly
ensnared in no end of difficulties. Inspired by the Church's
courageous stand and driven by loyalty to conscience and
calling, upwards of 90 per cent of Norway's 14,000
teachers resigned almost immediately from the Nazi

Laerersamband, leaving it entirely ineffectual for Quisling's purposes. Similarly people of other professions withdrew from the organizations which the Nazis had prescribed for them. The result was a complete crack-up of the Quisling program and the war's most significant victory for Norway's home front. In a fit of rage and despair Quisling stood before a group of adamant teachers on May 22nd and screamed: "You are spoiling the game for me!"

Quisling's "game" was in fact spoiled, but the victory had not been achieved without cost. Mounting circumstances during the spring months of 1942 had brought about the resignations of the bishops, deans, and virtually all the clergymen of the State Church of Norway; these resignations applied only to "official" relations with the State and explicitly did not affect the clergymen's spiritual duties to their congregations or their relations with one another. The Norwegian State Church became a "free Church," carrying on independently of the Nazi government in power.

In retaliation for the home front's resistance, the Nazis made thousands of arrests. In this the Church's highest leaders were not spared. Bishop Berggrav, for instance, was placed in a concentration camp and later transferred to "house arrest"—a term used to describe his present confinement in a small cottage; there he is under constant heavy guard, and he is allowed no contact whatsoever with the outside world. Schools were discontinued for weeks, and nearly 2,000 teachers were arrested; hundreds of these were later put to hard labor in the desolate regions of northern Norway. The arrests of countless other persons taxed the capacity of Norwegian concentration camps and necessitated the establishment of many new ones. The frequent executions of Norwegians during the spring months of 1942 by German firing squads were not unrelated to the home front's unyielding opposition to the new Minister-President Quisling and his sinister scheming.

All in all, the stand made by the Norwegian home front during the turbulent months of February, March and April, 1942, will constitute one of the proudest pages in the long history of Norway, and it will never be forgotten that in the struggle which then took place the Church fulfilled its rôle as leader and protector of the people.

The "State Act at Akershus"

Two events combined to make Sunday, February 1, 1942, a day of outstanding significance in the records of Norway under German occupation. On that day, at the ancient Akershus Castle in Oslo, Vidkun Quisling was proclaimed "Minister-President" of Norway. At almost the same hour in Trondheim Nazi police were blocking the doors of Nidaros Cathedral where a service was about to begin; it marked the first time in modern Norwegian history that members of a congregation had been prevented from worshipping in their own church. Each of these events touched off a series of others which gradually merged into a rapidly swelling stream.

The affair at Akershus was in the approved Hitlerian pattern and was accompanied with much pomp and ceremony. Reichskommissar Josef Terboven, on behalf of the German government, conferred upon Quisling his new title and authority. But the populace was not there to applaud and cheer. The people of Oslo did not go near Akershus that day; they disregarded orders to display flags and they refused to ride on street cars decorated with bunting in honor of Quisling.

Populace or no populace, Reichskommissar Terboven made a speech, and he devoted an important part of it to a stern attack on Bishop Berggrav who just at that time was lying ill in a hospital.

Terboven declared the Bishop had played a very important rôle in "the old system," and he spoke of Berggrav's visits to Berlin and London after the conclusion of the Polish campaign. The Bishop had written down the conversations he had held at that time with Field Marshal Goering, former Foreign Minister Lord Halifax, and the Archbishop of Canterbury, and Terboven announced that the original manuscript was now in his possession. He read certain excerpts from it.

Bearing in mind that "the Devil may cite Scripture to prove his purpose," it is only necessary to say here that Germany's highest representative in Norway drew the conclusion that Bishop Berggrav's "unambiguous and undeniable opinion" was that Germany's occupation of Norway was "not only morally and politically justified, but was also a military duty dictated by self-preservation." Continued Terboven: "According to Berggrav, England was an enemy and Germany a friend of Norway's neutrality."

Terboven charged that although Berggrav had revealed

himself as "the unreserved witness of the absolute right-
ness of Nasjonal Samling's policy," he nevertheless remained silent when it came to adopting that policy as his
own. "Whether it is due to fear of the people, to vanity,
or to an un-Christian and probably insuperable enmity for
Germany; or whether it is due to a mixture of all of these,
I am unable to judge," continued Terboven. "But that is
absolutely of no account. He may well continue to remain
silent, but he must then also remain silent on all political
questions!"

That Terboven should have devoted so much of his
speech to a denunciation of Berggrav was in itself no
small tribute to the man who already stood out as one of
the chief obstacles to Nazism in Norway. Before the month
was out Berggrav had supplied abundant evidence that in
this respect, at least, Terboven had judged him correctly.

The Affair at Trondheim

Detailed accounts from Norway give a dramatic picture
of the happenings at Trondheim on Sunday, February 1st,
when thousands were barred by Nazi police from attending services in the city's historic cathedral.

The facts in the case were these: The Rev. Arne Fjellbu,
Dean of the Trondheim Cathedral, and one of the most
respected of Norwegian clergymen, was to speak at the
Cathedral at the regular Sunday morning worship on
February 1st. On January 26th the Nazi Minister of
Church and Education suddenly wired instructions to the
Bishop of Trondheim, Johan Nicolai Stören, ordering
him to open the church on February 1st to the Rev. Bless-

ing Dahle, one of the very few ministers in Norway who have turned Nazi.

In spite of protests by Bishop Stören and Dean Fjellbu against this violation of law and traditions, the instructions were insisted upon and Blessing Dahle spoke at the so-called "festival services" at eleven o'clock in the morning. His topic was the now famous "State Act" which took place the same day at Akershus Castle in Oslo and at which Major Vidkun Quisling assumed the title and duties of "Minister-President" of Norway with German blessings. Only a meager audience of local Nazis attended the service conducted by Blessing Dahle.

Meanwhile the service to be conducted by Dean Fjellbu had been postponed until two o'clock in the afternoon. By the time Dahle's service was over, large crowds were streaming towards the Cathedral, and a considerable number of persons were already seated in the church when police marched up to prevent any more from entering. It was to enforce this order that police clubs were brought into play.

An Eye-Witness Account

A man who was present that afternoon has supplied the following eye-witness account of the happenings at Trondheim Cathedral:

"It was no unruly mob, but thousands of Christians. Among them was nearly the entire clergy of Trondheim. They were standing outside the Cathedral, prevented by police from entering the House of God to listen to the service and to receive Holy Communion.

"That half-hour will be a most precious memory of the most serious times in which we are now living. We were freezing, but we could not leave the place. We had to find some expression for what we felt. We did not make a noise like an ordinary crowd of demonstrators.

"From the most easterly part of the place I suddenly heard a voice, I do not know whose, starting Luther's old hymn. All of us took off our hats and joined in the singing of 'A mighty fortress is our God, a trusty shield and weapon . . . strong mail of craft and power, He weareth in this hour; on earth is not His equal.'

"While we were standing there with uniformed and armed policemen in front of us, the old song carried by thousands of voices sounded prouder and mightier than any I have ever heard. Then came Blix's 'National Hymn' and after that Norway's national anthem. Nobody said a word. I was standing almost in front of the crowd beside some girls fifteen to twenty years old. When I looked at them I saw that they were weeping. And all of us had difficulties in keeping back our tears.

"When Bishop Stören came out of the church and asked the crowd to leave without incident they finally did so. Meanwhile Dean Fjellbu addressed those who had entered the church before the police marched onto the scene."

Dean Fjellbu's Sermon

Dean Fjellbu based his sermon on the regular text for the day, Matthew 19: 27-30: "Peter said to Jesus: 'We have left everything and followed you.' " As he spoke, the

Dean doubtlessly realized it was the last sermon he would preach in a Norwegian church for some time to come. Shortly after the service he was "dismissed" from his office.

With deep sorrow (declared Dean Fjellbu in his sermon), God looks at those who are thinking according to the opportunistic view. The devil always tries tricks to make us take care of ourselves instead of performing the will of God. When God tells us what he demands, the devil is whispering into our ears: "Be careful!" The devil is whispering into the ears of Civil Service employees and other employees: "You may risk being dismissed." The devil is whispering into the ears of merchants and others: "You may risk losing your customers."

But Jesus speaks to those who have left house, brothers and sisters, parents and children, or property for His name.

Have we left everything? I do not think, first of all, of the visible things which we can leave. It is possible "to live in castles and to nevertheless have left everything; it is possible to live in a humble hut and yet have sacrificed very little."

In the first place I am thinking of that which makes the spirit and the will free. What really matters is to join the cause of Christ and God in such a way that you can sacrifice everything when asked without getting anything in return, without expecting any reward.

In these serious times we have to be confident that everything shall become new. Follow Jesus!

I often think of what will happen when the war is over. I remember the years after the last war. Hope lived that everything would become new. Between these two wars ideologies had their springtime. And these ideologies had as their aim that everything should become new. But now we must have learned that nothing becomes new if we are not following Jesus, if we are not letting our ideologies be decided by the spirit and might of Christ.

Only when the Son of Man sits on His glittering throne do all things become new. Towards that goal we shall work. To reach that goal is worth leaving everything.

But who shall govern in the new times to come? Only those who are not thinking of what they are going to receive in return, who are not seeking anything for themselves, their party, or their class. Not selfish people but wholehearted warriors of Christ. Will you be one of them? The chance to follow Jesus is free to all classes, nations and races.

After the service Bishop Stören declared police had violated the law and the freedom of the church in preventing members of the congregation from attending. Skancke replied that the service had been prohibited because it constituted a demonstration against Nasjonal Samling, Quisling's political party.

The "Ungdomsfylking" Law

On February 6th the new Quisling government held its first meeting. Ensconced in the King's Chair at the Royal Palace, and surrounded by his all-Nazi cabinet, the Minister-President at last assumed his cherished rôle as Norway's "Little Hitler." At this and later meetings he announced new laws—many of them. But the two which brought the sharpest repercussions were those affecting the children of the nation and their teachers.

In decreeing, February 6th, that all children between the ages of 10 and 18 years must become members of the *Ungdomsfylking,* Nazi youth organization, Quisling acted cautiously. He announced all the children would have to "do service" in the organization, but did not specify when or where or for how long that "service" would have to be performed. In fact, he did not describe the nature of it and even allowed intimations to creep in that it would be for only brief periods annually. In all likelihood he was trying to make the new law appear almost harmless in its effects—so harmless that the people would not find it worth the time or trouble to object.

Another good reason for Quisling's "pussyfooting" was the children themselves. From his point-of-view they had, up to then, been highly un-co-operative. By and large, the youngsters had been openly fearless and defiant of the Germans and the Norwegian Nazis. They jeered uniformed men on the streets, and they staged school strikes in all parts of Norway to show their contempt for the New Order. They concocted countless symbols, insignia, and gestures with which to demonstrate their loyalty to King Haakon. The children who, due to parental pressure or by their own choice, paraded as Nazis, were ostracized by the others and often severely beaten.

Quisling also had the parents to reckon with; he knew that about 99 out of every 100 persons were opposed to his leadership. And there were also the teachers and clergymen who might become aroused if they suspected infringements were being made on the provinces which law and tradition had assigned to them. No wonder Quisling thought it best to content himself with a finger at first, later to seize the whole hand.

But cautious as he was, Quisling was not cautious enough. Led by the ever-vigilant bishops of the Church of Norway, the whole country rose in a violent storm of protest against the *Ungdomsfylking* law.

The Bishops Take Up the Fight

The bishops, although gravely concerned with the events that transpired in Trondheim on February 1st, temporarily turned their attention away from that matter to face this new menace—the prospect of children being torn away from the Christian influence of home, church, and school in order to be molded in the Nazi pattern. Accordingly, they assembled at Oslo on February 14th and drew up a sharp letter of protest to Ragnar Skancke, Quisling's Minister of Church and Education, who had been requested by Quisling to "help formulate" the law which was to become effective March 1st.

The text of the bishops' letter follows:

The basic relationship between parents and children is a dispensation of the Creator, a God-stressed relationship which prevails inviolable and sacred for all homes.

The responsibility and the right which therein are given to the home, are therefore unconditional and indissoluble.

At the baptism of a child the responsibility for the bringing up of the child is placed upon the parent. The children's school is a mutually arranged means of aid in this upbringing and the first paragraph of the school law states that the school's purpose is to assist in giving the children a Christian and moral education.

The homes and the church have therefore also a right to share in determining the policies of the school, and the parents have in certain circumstances a right to take their children out of school. The school has no authority against the baptismal obligations nor against the Fourth Commandment.

Every father and mother also holds full responsibility for how they have permitted others to take part in forming their children's character, faith and conviction. This conscientious responsibility places not only a duty on the parents but also gives them an inviolable right.

In the same way the Fourth Commandment, "honor thy father and thy mother," is for the children not alone a duty but a right given them by God.

A good home's inner freedom has always been a foundation pillar in our society and no one can by force break into a home and create antagonism between parents and children without God's commandment being trampled under foot.

In all this the church and the parents stand inseparably bound by their conscience and by God's command. He who would attempt to force the children out of the parents' bonds of responsibility and to disrupt the Divine right of the home, would at the same time be forcing the parents to the utmost act of conscience.

Every father and mother knows that they one time will stand answerable to the Almighty for how they have brought up or let others bring up their children. Here they must obey God more than man.

As the overseers of the Church, we recognize it as our duty to present this clearly and unmistakably upon the occasion of your having received orders to assist in the formation of a law aimed to compulsorily mobilize all children from the age of 9–10 years and upwards to an influence which countless parents must recognize as intolerable in relation to their conscientious obligations.

An intrusion of this kind will touch the people in their innermost and deepest life. To those who in their conscientious distress have turned to us in this matter we have for the present not been able to give any other answer than that we have sent you this remonstration. A copy of it is being sent simultaneously to Minister Axel Stang.

The letter was signed by the seven bishops: Eivind Berggrav, J. Stören, J. Maroni, Andreas Fleischer, Gabriel Skagestad, Henrik Hille, Wollert Krohn-Hansen.

Skancke's Reply to Bishops

Minister Skancke, in his reply to the bishops' letter, attempted to justify the government's position and in so doing disclosed that the *Ungdomsfylking* intended to "educate the children" in order to save the Norwegian people "from plunging over the precipice." His letter follows:

In their letter the bishops of the Church touch upon vital matters pertaining to home, school and church. The parents' responsibility for the children's upbringing in cooperation with church and school, and the children's duty to fall into line with the care of father and mother belong to the home's foundation pillars which cannot be torn down in a Christian land without the bitterest consequences.

It appears from the letter that the bishops have an open eye for the rights of parents and the parental authority and parental responsibility. But there appears to be a lack of understanding with Luther that in the "parental authority" all other authority has is roots.

In his explanation of the Fourth Commandment Luther comments at length on this point in his Large Catechism: "The same may be said of obedience due to civil authority, which authority, as we have said, is all embraced in the estate of fatherhood and extends beyond all other relations. Here the father is not one of a single family, but one of many tenants, citizens or subjects. Through civil rulers, as through our parents, God gives us food, home and land, protection and security. Therefore, since they bear this name and title with all honor as their chief glory, it is our duty to honor them and to esteem them as we would the greatest treasure and the most precious jewel on earth."

As the highest authority of a people the State has the greatest responsibility for, the greatest authority and the greatest right over every single citizen. This authority, responsibility and right of the State applies also "in the same way as the responsibility for the children's education is placed upon the parents," so is the responsibility for the people's education placed upon the State.

That this responsibility for our people, who have been neglected through many years, is especially great ought also to be clear to the bishops of the Church.

The State was ordained by God just as much as the family and just as much as the Church. The Church has no right to interfere with the State's right and duty to endeavor, on the basis of this, its responsibility, to solve its educational problem with regard to the people.

The State's view, then, is briefly this: If the Norwegian people are to be saved from plunging over the precipice, then the children must be saved.

If our Norwegian people are tomorrow to become a strong and healthy people who understand their times and will the good, then the children must learn to understand their times and will the good. It is for this that the Nasjonal Samling's *Ungdomsfylking,* with the National Youth Leader at the head, wants to educate the Norwegian children.

To call this compulsory mobilization only goes to show how little the Church's bishops themselves understand of the New Order. Now for once it is impossible to shut oneself out from the ground-breaking time of a people. It must inevitably result eventually in one's having shut himself out from the people themselves and in being left behind.

Last fall the *Ungdomsfylking* knocked on the Church's door when an effort was made to secure Our Savior's Church for a morning service. The Bishop of Oslo at that time took part in closing the Church door to the national youth. Did not the time have to come when the national youth closes the door to the Church's bishops?

The "Laerersamband"

Meanwhile another significant struggle was taking place in Norway—that of the teachers against the Quisling law of February 8th which "automatically" made all of them members of the new teachers' organization called the *Laerersamband*. As members, the law said, they would be compelled to make their teaching conform with Nazi precepts. Those who refused membership, it was declared, would be removed from their profession and put to "socially useful work in northern Norway, or elsewhere."

Faced with the choice of *Laerersamband* membership or labor service, the teachers chose the latter. By the hundreds and the thousands they sent their letters to the Department of Church and Education resigning from the Nazi organization. By mid-April it was definitely known that more than 12,000 of Norway's 14,000 teachers had thus withdrawn from what they knew to be a Nazi trap. The number may have been considerably greater.

It was not purely coincidental that the teachers and clergy should be fighting it out with the Nazis at one and the same time. In Norway Church and School have always been closely related. In the popular mind they are regarded as foundation pillars of Norwegian society. Both come under the jurisdiction of the government's Department of Church and Education. A fine spirit of co-operation has always existed between the two institutions. Children of Lutheran faith, for instance, receive their religious instruction in the schools, and frequently the community pastor serves as teacher for these classes. It is noteworthy that despite this close relationship, the Church has never sought to dominate or dictate the interests or activities of the schools. It is also significant that schoolmen have frequently been selected as members of the cabinet to head the Department of Church and Education.

Like the churchmen, the teachers were thoroughly alarmed over the possible results of the *Ungdomsfylking* law. Although their careers, economic security, and their lives were in danger because of the decree directed at them, the teachers were able to ignore their own peril for the moment and support the bishops in the protest against compulsory youth mobilization. This they did through their established organizations.

Obviously the Nazis had expected no such display of cool courage from the teachers, commonly supposed to be a docile lot. There is also evidence that they were confused by it. For a while Quisling and his aides hesitated, not knowing which way to turn. High-pressure propaganda and loud-voiced threats alike failed to halt the mass desertions of teachers from the *Laerersamband*. To the Nazis it finally became a matter of "saving face." Towards the end of February several arrests were made, and during March wholesale arrests became commonplace. By April 1st, nearly 2,000 teachers had been put in concentration camps.

The Nazis had declared only those who were members of the *Laerersamband* would be permitted to teach, but it soon became apparent that to carry out this threat would be the near equivalent of attempting to operate schools without teachers. Consequently, on February 26th the Nazis saw fit to announce that the schools throughout the country would remain closed for one month "because of the fuel shortage." The schools did not generally reopen until May 1st and, when they did, all non-arrested teachers were back at their jobs despite the fact that they had meanwhile made no peace or compromise with the Nazis.

School Strike Threatened

Another factor that may have played a part in inducing the Nazis to announce the so-called "fuel shortage" vacation is indicated in the following message which was sent to *Laerersambandet* leaders on February 25th by an official of the Norwegian State Police:

From reliable sources I have received word that there is talk in the city about starting a school strike on March 1st. Presumably this would be as a demonstration against the law making young people subject to duty in Nasjonal Samling's *Ungdomsfylking* from that date on. If this should prove true, we apparently will be faced with a nationwide action, and for that reason I am notifying you about the above-mentioned rumors and at the same time politely request preventive measures.

During April, however, the Nazis had made good their threat to put "recalcitrant" teachers to "socially useful work." They had transported hundreds of them to northern Norway where they were used like slaves for loading and unloading of German ships and for the construction of German fortifications.

The Bishops Resign

The seven bishops of the Church of Norway had no intention of forgetting the outrages committed by the Nazis at the Trondheim Cathedral on February 1st. On February 23rd and 24th they reassembled at Oslo, and from that session emerged a document which each of the bishops signed and sent individually to the Nazi Department of Church and Education. It was a letter of resignation. The text is as follows:

On Sunday, February 1st, it happened that the State authorities, under protest from responsible leaders of the Church, forced the Dean in Trondheim away from his morning service and imposed another to conduct the service.

The man whom the Department "for special reasons" forced in, Pastor Blessing Dahle, himself declared in writing to the Dean that there could not be any full service inasmuch as it would not be fitting to hold communion.

That this could not be a congregational service is also apparent from newspaper accounts of how the "Hird's" black banner was placed in the church choir along with the sun-cross emblem and Nasjonal Samling's red-and-yellow flag.

With the known suspense which today prevails among the people—a situation which the Department has on an earlier occasion characterized as a sad fact—the single factor that political symbols are brought into a church constitutes a breach of the peace which is to prevail during a congregational service.

The Dean therefore announced that his congregational service with communion would be held at two o'clock in the afternoon. To do so he had both the clear right and churchly duty. After the pastor and a goodly number of church-goers already were inside the church and while others were streaming towards it, the police suddenly stepped in and locked the church doors, forced those approaching the church to withdraw; yes, even the police patrol car was used against the orderly congregation members. Despite this no demonstrations resulted. The congregation sang some hymns as they stood there before the church gates blocked by police.

In this affair there have occurred three unheard-of intrusions of the Church's and congregation's right: first, the State authorities have violated the Church's routine and deprived the congregation and its pastor of the morning service.

In a circular letter of February 2nd the Department stated that one "presumably" is entitled to this. By this expression the Department has itself supplied the words for the uncertainty of even the formal right—if it exists at all.

But the Department had closed its eyes to the realities.

Not under any condition could the Department without the most flagrant breach of the Church's routine, undertake such a fundamental decision without first placing the matter before the bishops.

Still more important, if the Department of Church and Education should at all be supposed to have a formal right to deprive the congregation of its service, then this could only be on clear, churchly motives. The congregation's Sunday service with accompanying communion is a central and fundamental part of the congregation's devotional life.

According to the constitution the state leader, who has anything at all to do with the church services, is required to profess our religion and to *enforce* and protect it.

Therefore, consideration for the preaching of the gospel and the upbuilding of the congregation should be the deciding factor everywhere where the State exercises a directional authority on the basis of our religious belief. The State has in itself no special considerations to assert here. If the State does this the basic feature of our Church is shattered.

In addition to this, the law placed upon a congregation's pastor the duty to hold his service. This duty is placed upon him for the congregation's sake. . . . The pastor is tied to the congregation by far stronger bonds than the legal ones, namely by the responsibility and the conscientious obligation which his calling places upon him. If he is to be excused or forced away from doing his duty it is only regard for the congregation's benefit which rightly can be taken into account. Pastor and congregation and devotional services are inviolable both in their sacred solidarity and in their legally and constitutionally protected right.

The bishops are compelled to record that the State, by that which has happened in Trondheim, has misused its entrusted assignment as Church administrator in order to shove consideration for the Church aside for the benefit of that which the Department calls special considerations of State or political nature.

Thereby the State has broken its obligation with regard to the Church.

Secondly, this impression becomes tremendously increased by the dramatic method whereby the Church Department also sought to destroy the devotional service for the congregation which its pastor had announced for the afternoon.

Through a local party member the Department allowed police to get instructions to prevent the Dean's service without any effort being made by the Department to notify the bishop and pastor about what was to take place.

In these times we have the experience that the congregation which seeks God's house is chased away by armed State authorities.

Thirdly, the extreme limits are reached when the Church sees that the Department of Church and Education, far from reprimanding the police for this, places the blame on the presiding pastor and without warning *dismisses* Dean Fjellbu from his office. He has the clear words of the law on his side. Upon his service as a pastor there can be cast no shadow of stain. He has the full respect and confidence of his congregation and his superiors, also in his capacity as the bishop's substitute.

After having gotten the case fully clarified the Church Department, instead of protecting the Church's and congregation's right to worship God, chose brutally to permit its minister, who has done his churchly duty, to be dismissed.

The Norwegian Church's bishops would be unfaithful to their calling if they continued to co-operate with an administration which in this manner, without trace of churchly reason, invades the rights of the congregation and even adds injustice to might. *So I submit that I hereby resign from the conduct of my office.*

That is to say: I now divest myself of that which the State has deputed to me. The spiritual duty, assigned to me through ordination at the Lord's altar, is still mine with God and with right. To be a preacher of the Word, supervisor of the congregation and spiritual advisor of the pastors is and will continue to be my calling. I will in the future look after this so far as it is possible for a non-official to do so.

But to continue the administrative co-operation which exercises might against the Church would be to betray the most sacred trust.

With Luther we have tried in our service to be loyal to the authorities as far as word and commandment permitted. But as it came for Luther so also it comes for us, the moment when we must follow our conviction and assert the Church's rights against the State's injustice.

Forms of government may change, but with its Church father the Church knows that against what Luther called tyranny stands God himself in his Word and with His spirit's power.

Woe unto us if we did not here obey God more than man.

To every pastor and congregation under his jurisdiction each of the bishops sent a copy of the above letter with this annotation:

In accordance with the position which the bishoprics hold among the congregations and clergy, we find it our duty to re-

port to you that we have today felt compelled to resign from
the conduct of our offices. The occurrences which in the end
left us no choice if we were to remain true to our convictions
will be made clear to you by the letter which we today have
sent to the Department of Church and Education.

We greet congregations and pastors with thanks for all the
loyalty which has been shown our Norwegian Church. Be calm
and truthful. Oppose all recklessness, all falsehood and all hate.
We shall build Norway in love. The same spirit be in you as
was in Jesus Christ when he said: "Have salt in yourself and
be at peace with one another." We shall continue to stand with
you in praying and working for God's cause among these, our
people, also after we—as you now will learn—no longer are
able to remain in our offices.

CHAPTER VIII

QUISLING AS "NORWAY'S SUPREME BISHOP"

WHEN QUISLING, by the so-called "State Act at Aker-shus," became Minister-President he boasted of having taken over the earlier functions of both the King, Storting, and Government. According to the Constitution, the King is Norway's supreme bishop. Thus, according to the new set-up, Quisling had become a sort of fuehrer-bishop. His most willing "church tool," Sigmund Feyling, made this clear in a speech broadcast on March 27th. He declared:

The fact that Quisling is now considered Norway's supreme bishop will have far-reaching consequences. The New Order will naturally exercise influence upon the Church which in the future will gain a greater national significance than ever before. The goal is the introduction of a Norwegian Christianity, and the Church must open its eyes to racial consciousness and living-space. If the Norwegian Christian front wishes less freedom, then its present attitude will bring about the desired result.

During the days preceding this speech Quisling had already been making full use of his new churchly fuehrer-eminence. After the bishops had sent in their resignations of February 24th he had stripped Bishop Berggrav of "titles and eminence."

On the very day he had submitted his resignation Berggrav received the following telegram from the Department of Church and Education:

Your letter of the 24th instant wherein you resign from conduct of your office has been received. The reasons given in the letter are to a large extent not in agreement with the real facts of the case which you yourself should be well acquainted with. Your resignation will be dealt with at the government meeting next Thursday. The Department meanwhile regards you as being suspended from your office as of today and has turned the conduct of your office over to the dean concerned. The Department at the same time prohibits any kind of continuation of your official duties in any form whatsoever after you in this way resigned from the conduct of your office. The Norwegian canon law does not permit such clerical supervisory authority in the Norwegian Church outside the regular bishopric.

On February 27th the following brief article appeared in the Nazi-controlled press under the small, one-line heading: "Relieved of Duty:"

OSLO TODAY—Following the compromising information which has come to light regarding Bishop Berggrav's political activity, he—through employment of an extraneous excuse—reported to the Department of Church and Education on February 24th that he was resigning from his office.

In this connection, at a meeting of the government held the 26th instant, Mr. Berggrav has been relieved of his duties as bishop without right to official title. Mr. Berggrav must from now on be regarded as a private individual.

Furthermore, Quisling had summoned Berggrav to a hearing at the Palace during which he tried to find a purely political reason for "cracking down" on his opponent. He tried, namely, to get Berggrav to "confess" to what he called "the crime which shall never be forgotten." He was referring to the replacement of the first Quisling government, only a few days after its creation in April, 1940, by the Administrative Council which lasted until September 25, 1940.

More specifically, Quisling wanted Berggrav to "confess" that it was he and Paal Berg, chief justice of the Norwegian Supreme Court, who had taken the initiative in overthrowing his first government after it had been in power only a few days following the arrival of the Germans in April, 1940. The Administrative Council was made up, for the most part, of men who were loyal to the King and to the country's democratic traditions; their aim was to make the best out of a bad situation.

In reality it was at the written request of the German Minister, Dr. Bräuer, that Berggrav had collaborated in setting up the Administrative Council. Prominent members of the Nasjonal Samling also assisted. The Bräuer letter was naturally a source of embarrassment to Quisling; it was proof that his own German overlords lacked confidence in him and wanted his government deposed. Obviously Quisling could not hope to prosecute Berggrav on purely political grounds until the letter was destroyed. But his efforts to obtain it had been of no avail; not even a police search of the Berggrav home had produced it.

At their meeting in the Palace Quisling demanded that Berggrav supply the names of others who had aided in forming the Administrative Council. Berggrav again refused, although he added that he could name two "prominent Nasjonal Samling members" who had taken part. But Quisling did not care to pursue the point further.

Thereupon Berggrav seized his advantage and turned the tables on Quisling by assuming the rôle of interrogator. He wanted to know how Quisling could have falsified his (Berggrav's) letter of resignation by allowing newspapers to state that he had been dismissed.

"We in Nasjonal Samling see it that way," answered Quisling.

"Then I have nothing to do here," said Berggrav.

"You triple traitor!" bellowed Quisling. "You deserve having your head chopped off!"

"Well, here I am," answered the Bishop.

Quisling Explains the Crisis

On February 26th Quisling sent to all pastors of the State Church a lengthy "explanation" of the Church situation. It opened with a vitriolic attack on the Church leadership in general and on Bishop Berggrav in particular. Quisling wrote:

It has been a misfortune for Norway and especially for the Norwegian Church that at the head of this organization through these fateful years have stood certain small men, modern pharisees and traitor-bishops, who from first to last have conducted themselves more like worldly party-politicians than as true servants of the Church, and who have drawn many weak souls with them. By their cunning and intrigue they have not only disgraced the Church's and Christianity's cause, but have also greatly damaged the vital political and economic interests of the Norwegian people. Instead of preaching peace and reconciliation in the spirit of Christianity, they have regarded their task as that of creating unrest and maintaining domestic strife and national disunity and disruption. One of them, Bishop Berggrav, must bear the chief blame for having brought tremendous moral and material losses and sufferings upon the Norwegian people. . . . When Berggrav felt the ground burning beneath him, he spared nothing to draw the other bishops with him in order to thus cover up his own actions.

Quisling then continued with his own version of the latest crisis in the Church conflict. He blamed the bishops for having chosen the path of brutal action, thereby placing themselves outside their positions as supervisors in the Norwegian Church. He placed the entire responsibility for the incident at the Trondheim Cathedral on Dean Fjellbu who, he charged, had planned the afternoon worship for the purpose of making a political demonstration "instead of respecting the Department's devotions at Trondheim Cathedral on Sunday, February 1st, a special service arranged in conjunction with the national festival day, and which naturally was open to all just as a regular church service." Regarding the dismissal of Dean Fjellbu, Quisling wrote: "All that needs be said about this is that the Dean had also previously misused his clerical position for political purposes. His dismissal would have taken place even though this latest insubordination had not occurred."

Quisling closed his "pastoral letter" with lengthy assurances of Nasjonal Samling's innocence in the Church conflict. He declared it was "the Church's bishops and their shady followers" who made use of every opportunity to create strife, and who had acted "not in the spirit of love and reconciliation, but in the spirit of hate, for which

Christ allowed Himself to be nailed to the Cross in order that it might be taken out of the world."

The Deans Resign

On the same day that Quisling's letter was sent out all deans of the Church resigned. The day before they had received orders to substitute for the "suspended" bishops, and their joint resignation was their reply to that order. On February 26th a number of other events also occurred. The bishops were ordered to report to the police twice a day—an order which was later rescinded because of the "dangerous" effect upon the clergy. On that day, too, the pastors of Oslo and the vicinity took action. About ninety of them sent individual letters to the Department of Church and Education stating that they agreed with their bishop and deans, and that they would recognize only Berggrav as their bishop and supervisor.

The result of Quisling's activities as self-appointed supreme bishop was that the beginning of March, 1942, found the Norwegian State Church without bishops or deans, and pastors and congregations on the point of departure, ready to follow their leaders. On March 4th Quisling produced a temporary amendment to the Church laws giving the Department of Church and Education authority to appoint pastors, other than the deans, to a vacant bishopric, and to transfer the duties of the dean to another pastor in the diocese when conditions made this necessary. That done, the Minister-President began making appointments.

As acting Dean and Bishop for Oslo Diocese he named

the Rev. H. Hagen of Bekkelaget; for Hamar Diocese, the Rev. G. Falck-Hansen of Grue; for Agder Diocese, the Rev. Chr. Hansteen of Herefoss; for Stavanger Diocese, the Rev. H. Kvasnes of Höyland; for Björgvin Diocese, the Rev. D. Zwilgmeyer of Fana; for Nidaros Diocese, the Rev. Einar Lothe of Hadsel; for Haalogaland Diocese, the Rev. J. Sivertsen of Hammerfest. With the exception of Lothe, all the new "bishops" remained in their regular parishes, carrying on their new duties from there. All of the appointees were known to be members of Nasjonal Samling, but it soon developed that not even among his own followers could Quisling be sure of complete allegiance to his Church policies. Pastor Hansteen, a brother-in-law of the late Gulbrand Lunde, Quisling's Propaganda Minister, and who for years had been an active Nazi, refused to accept his appointment in Agder Diocese and simultaneously advised a complete change in Nasjonal Samling's Church policies. Shortly afterwards Quisling issued a new law dividing Agder Diocese in two; the westerly part was added to the Stavanger Diocese, and the other was reorganized into a new Skien Diocese with the Rev. Ludvig Daae Zwilgmeyer as acting dean and bishop. Thereby Hansteen was swept neatly and painlessly out of the picture.

The Pastors Resign

It now depended upon the attitude of the clergy as to whether the newly appointed "acting bishops" were going to be able to function at all. The first warning of this attitude had appeared when the pastors of Oslo and vicinity spoke up and said they would recognize no one but Berg-grav. The authorities tried to quell this "sign of revolt" by dismissing ten pastors in Oslo Diocese, including the Rev. Ingvald B. Carlsen, depriving them of "titles and eminence," and prohibiting them from participating in any Church work in the future. When Sigmund Feyling was asked on what legal basis this action was taken, he replied by referring to decree of October 4, 1940, which states that all those who do not work positively for the New Order are subject to dismissal.

The Church Front was all too firmly welded to be disrupted, any more than the teachers' front, by threats and terror. Under the leadership of the Christian Council a united action was launched among the combined clergy. The pastors wrote to the Department of Church and Education stating that for reasons of conscience they were compelled to resign from their offices. They maintained that they would continue to carry on that work in their congregations which could be done by non-officials in accordance with the Holy Scriptures, the Confession of Faith, and the Altar Book.

The pastors further maintained that they could accept no directions as to how God's Word should be preached during present circumstances. They said they considered ordination a lifetime call, and were therefore in disagreement with the view that an ordained pastor could, for political and worldly reasons, be deprived of his position and his duty of preaching the Word and administering the sacraments. Nor could his clerical robes be taken from him, because they belong to the Church alone.

Finally it was declared in the letter to the Department that the Church stood guard over the Christian schools, the Christian homes, the Christian volunteer work, and the Christian social welfare work. Moral education of children without regard for Christian considerations was protested against. The pastors made it clear that they were obliged to obey the Bible in all worldly matters which were in conflict with demands of the authorities. They maintained that the Church's properties and possessions did not belong to the State but to the still functioning Christian Church in the people. "The Evangelical Lutheran Church," concluded the letter, "is today as for earlier generations, our spiritual fatherland."

The reasons for the pastors' resignations were explained in a longer document * which all pastors, participating in the action, read from their pulpits before beginning their sermons on Easter morning (April 5th). In other words, the document was read to all congregations of the Norwegian State Church with the exception of the very few presided over by Nazi-minded pastors and an additional few in remote sections of northernmost Norway where difficulties of communication stood in the way of concerted action. The report ended with these words:

As the servant of the Church and this congregation, I have today placed this matter before you, and I simultaneously state that my continued service will depend on to what extent the Church's view on this [the responsibility for the people's education] and other questions which have been under discussion is respected.

* "The Foundations of the Church." See Appendix, page 172.

The Rise of a "Free" Church

In a nut shell, this action meant that the Church was declaring itself independent of the State and was turning to the establishment of a free people's Church—unless the authorities altered their policies. This was no new idea in the history of the Norwegian Church. It had been discussed for many years prior to the war and had its strong spokesmen, but as long as the State fully respected the Church's rights and did not meddle with its inner workings, the advantages of maintaining a State Church had been so many and so great that the question of a separation appeared to have little chance of materializing. Now, however, the idea of a free people's Church was forcing itself upon the churchmen as the only solution to a difficult situation.

Above all, the new free Church was to have the form of a Church for spiritual guidance, in which the pastors could continue to perform the most important work of their calling, such as conducting divine services, baptizing children, officiating at funerals, and administering the sacraments of the altar. The only question was whether the Nazis would accept this emancipation of the Church—and if not, how far they would dare go to prevent it.

Apparently this action took the Nazis by surprise, and the authorities promptly branded it as an act of rebellion— a sort of declaration of war. Immediately there arose rumors of the most severe retaliatory measures, first and foremost against the responsible leaders. They and their followers were to be struck down without regard. The immediate reply of the Department of Church and Education to the pastors' statement was a telegraphed ultimatum to the effect that if they had not reported their willingness to resume their work in the State Church by 2 P.M. on Saturday, April 11th, they would face being dismissed within the next few days. Everybody knew that the pastors would not yield to the ultimatum. Later it was ascertained that only two out of approximately 700 pastors withdrew their resignations because of the ultimatum. But it was also known that the pastors would attempt to conduct services as usual in the churches on Sunday, April 12th, and the prospect of Nazi interference with those services caused great tension throughout the country.

Quisling and his gangsters were prepared to carry their fight against the churchmen to any extreme, even to the point of invading the churches and arresting the "rebellious" pastors for "activity hostile to people and State." On April 9th he had ordered the arrest of Bishop Berggrav together with four other leaders of the Christian Council: Ragnvald A. Indreboe, Ingvald B. Carlsen, H. E. Wisloeff and Chr. Hanssen. All but Hanssen were pastors. The Christian Council had publicly acknowledged responsibility for the letter which was read in the churches on Easter and which Nasjonal Samling regarded as an act of rebellion.

The Germans, however, apparently did not find this intensification of the Church conflict politically advisable, and they looked for means of allowing it to abate. For the time being, at least, no mass arrests of pastors were undertaken. The divine services of April 12th transpired without disturbance by the police. From German authorities came word that no further measures should be taken against the Church, and after a week had passed Quisling was forced to release Berggrav from the concentration camp. This must have been a rather painful defeat for the Minister-President, judging from the "explanation" supplied to the Oslo correspondent of *Stockholms Tidningen* by Sverre Riisnaes, the Nazi Minister of Justice. He declared: "Quisling still regards Berggrav as one guilty of high treason, but called off court proceedings against him in accordance with a law which permits authorities to take the public interest into consideration when they decide whether a case is to be prosecuted or not."

Quisling Opposed to a "Free" Church

The idea of a free people's Church rising entirely independent of the State is contradictory to the plans of Vidkun Quisling who has been trying to align all groups and organizations of Norwegian society under the State. Therefore he began placing all possible hindrances in the path of the new development, and when these proved ineffective he went so far as to offer compromises.

Faced with the prospect of a shortage of pastors for his "nazified" Church, Quisling hurriedly proclaimed a new law on April 7th authorizing the appointment of "mission leaders, American-educated ministers and qualified laymen with no theological training" to the regular pastorates. As it turned out, however, the "resigned" pastors continued to hold services and to minister to their congregations.

Another and more serious danger also faced him. It was that the departure of the pastors from the State Church would result immediately in the mass resignations of members with the result that Quisling would be left with a State Church that was nothing but an empty shell. To prevent this turn of events he proclaimed still another law in mid-April. It was in the form of an "amendment" to the Dissenters' Law, which allows Norwegian citizens to withdraw from the State Church in order to enter a Church of their own choosing. Quisling's amendment provided that all resignations from the State Church, in order to be valid, must be signed by a "competent" bishop.

It was clear that by a "competent" bishop was meant a "Quisling bishop," and that meant the threatened exodus from State Church membership was blocked. The method here employed is strongly reminiscent of that employed by Quisling's Minister of Justice, Sverre Riisnaes, and other high Norwegian Nazis, in obtaining listeners for their speech-making. Without warning they have frequently entered theaters or assembly halls, ordered police to lock all doors so that no one could leave, and then mounted the platform to deliver their harangue. Now the doors of the State Church had similarly been locked, shutting 96 per cent of the Norwegian population inside. What kind of religious life the Nazi authorities hoped to create through such methods is difficult to understand. In the light of the completely anti-Christian character and cultural nihilism of Nazism, however, the whole system of destruction is clear as the noonday sun. And in the second of these "laws" lies a Nazi confession which is well worth noting. A Church with Quisling as the supreme bishop can exist only in the form of a prison.

The situation resulting from these two "laws" might have produced grave consequences, and may still do so. The fact that the Germans stepped in to stay Quisling's hand led to a "breathing spell," during which pressure and violence gave way to "peace proposals" and bids of compromise.

CHAPTER IX

THE NAZIS SEEK A COMPROMISE

IMMEDIATELY UPON seeing the defeat of their plan to prevent "resigned" pastors from conducting services in their churches, the Nazis came forward with a plan for peace. They proposed the formation of a committee of six members, charging it with the task of working out a solution. Three of the members were to be Nasjonal Samling men and the others were to represent the "opposition." The Nazis went so far as to name all six members, but from the outset were doomed to failure, and it is doubtful if the committee ever convened. The loyal pastors of Norway were in no mood for compromise.

A few days later there was talk of another peace bid. The Nazis were then reported to have offered to revoke their appointments of the so-called "acting bishops," also dubbed "Quisling bishops," and to place in their stead some of the deans who had declared themselves to be fully in sympathy with Berggrav and the other resigned bishops. One condition of this plan was that the deans selected for the bishoprics would have to pledge their loyalty to the Quisling regime. No more was ever heard of this scheme.

The Seven-Point Appeal

Further indication of the abject position of the Nazis in relation to the Church conflict was provided by a 7-point appeal sent out by the new Quisling-appointed bishops on June 2nd. It is interesting because of its false presumptions (such as that the clergy is "on strike" and that its opposition to the Quisling government is for political reasons), its tricky reasoning, and its final outburst of "magnanimity" — a big-hearted "willingness-to-forgive-and-forget" which could fool no one. It is revealing, also, because it constitutes a disclosure by the Nazis of how strong and widespread the opposition actually is. The Norwegian Information Office in London learned that publication of the original version of this appeal was prohibited and various alterations were ordered. The original version, for instance, referred to the opposition as "an overwhelming part of our country's clergy"; this was changed to "some of our clergy."

Following is the text of the Quisling bishops' appeal as broadcast by the Oslo radio on July 1st and heard in the United States:

First, the Bible and our religious beliefs confirm that anyone opposing the authorities opposes the Order of God. In the Epistle to the Romans, 13th chapter, authorities are defined as being anyone with governing powers over a country which has been given to them by the grace of God. *Secondly,* there are the examples of Jesus and the apostles. Jesus and the apostles obeyed the heathen authorities of their time. As for the present government of Norway, it has continuously stated that it is on the side of Christianity and the Norwegian Church. This ought to be sufficient reason for us to support it unanimously in our fight for the country and the people. *Thirdly,* there is the limit to our obedience toward the authorities. The only written exception to obedience to authorities is found in the Book of Revelation, in chapters 4 to 18, and 15 to 29 [references apparently confused]. If the authorities refuse to allow the preaching of the Gospel, thereby attacking the life of Jesus and His work, it is our Christian duty to obey God and not the people. A case like that of this chapter has not occurred while the present government has been in power. The *fourth* point is the real cause of the Church strike. We have realized that some of our clergy oppose the present government for political reasons. They have, among other things, refused to publish banns of marriage, to marry people, to answer the official correspondence, and so on. The clergy who are on strike are allowing themselves to be used as tools in an attack on the new government. *Fifth,* there is the boycott of the loyal clergymen [here this refers to pro-Nazi pastors]. When sections [!] of congregations in certain parts [!] of the country boycotted the clergy, they did so for political and not for religious reasons. The clergy who are being boycotted preach the same Gospel as the clergy who are on strike, and they have the same religious foundations. *Sixth,* there is the godless movement. This movement, which is to be found in all countries and within all political parties, cannot be blamed on the National Socialist government. The godless movement in this country is the fruit of the sins of earlier generations. *Seventh,* there is reconciliation. The present split within our country's Christian population is a sin against the Holy Brotherhood and a tragedy for our Church and our people. In accordance with Jesus, who told us to love each other and who gave his life for us, we stretch out our hands in reconciliation and peace for the benefit of our country and people.

The appeal was signed by the following Quisling-named bishops: Fröyland, Daae Zwilgmeyer, H. I. B. Kvasnes, Einar Lothe, K. H. Hagen, Dagfinn Zwilgmeyer, E. G. Kristian, Falck-Hansen and J. Sivertsen.

Offer of Back Salaries Fails

On June 13th a circular letter was sent to the clergy by the Department of Church and Education. In it the Nazis stooped to attempting to bribe the pastors into ending the conflict by offering them their back salaries as a reward. Since their resignations the clergy had not been receiving their pay from the State.

The letter stated that the Church "will be losing respect and ground" among the Norwegian people if the "abnormal conditions" continued. The letter charged that with the resigned bishops and the greater part of the clergy maintaining they had left their State offices but were retaining the duties given them by God, the Catholic conception of the ordination of the clergy was affected. This, continued the letter, was in sharp conflict with Luther's conception, and for substantiation it referred to Luther's main work, *To the Christian Nobility,* and to the book, *Martin Luther,* by Hjalmar Holmquist. The letter then appealed to all pastors to return to work and to carry out their State-given duties. It added that pastors might call for salaries due them before the beginning of the new fiscal year (July 1st), and stated further that the Department had no objection to the appointment of a delegation by the pastors, who regarded themselves as opposed to "the central Church authorities," for the purpose of taking up negotiations with the Department. If the lawlessness and confusion resulting from the clergy's resignations were brought to an end, the letter promised, the Department would do its utmost to solve "as far as possible" the present problems in a manner satisfactory to the Church. Finally the letter stated that, by and large, the Department, on the basis of the Minister-President's circular letter to the clergy of February 26th and his statement of April 6th regarding Nasjonal Samling and the Church, would guarantee for the Church "full freedom to preach the Gospel to the entire people and to administer the sacraments in accordance with Christ's instructions." The letter was signed by Ragnar Skancke, head, and Sigmund Feyling, secretary, of the Department.

Commenting on this development, the newspaper, *Stockholms Tidningen,* declared: "Luther's opinion that the Church must obey the State as long as the Church has the freedom to preach the Gospel without interference is correct, but this assumes the State is obeying the common law. This is not the case in Norway today where the Quisling Government regards itself above the law." The bishops, it will be remembered, based their resignations primarily on Nazi interference with a regular service at Trondheim.

The Christian Council Rejects Offer

Early in July the Christian Council, formed in the fall of 1940 and representing all Christian organizations in Norway, flatly rejected a more elaborate compromise plan worked out by Quisling and the Quisling-appointed Bishop Kvasnes of Stavanger. Its announced purpose was to bring to an end the "lawlessness and confusion" resulting from the resignations of the regular bishops, deans, and clergymen.

Couched in assurances that the Nazi Department of Church and Education would do everything possible to bring about a solution satisfactory to the Church, the plan proposed that Bishop Eivind Berggrav should be granted a professorship in theology at Oslo University; that Bishop J. Maroni, who resigned with Berggrav, should graciously withdraw in compliance with the old-age retirement law; that Bishops Fleischer, Hille, Krohn-Hansen, and Skagestad, all of whom resigned, should be returned to their offices. So far as is known, no provision was made for the seventh of the original bishops, Johan Stören of Trondheim.

In its reply, the Christian Council, which is headed by Professor O. Hallesby and Dean Hygen of Oslo, declared that it had hoped that any peace negotiations would be introduced by the cancellations of the two bishop ordinations which took place at an Oslo church on June 28th, and which raised new storms of indignation throughout Norway. Both of the bishops inaugurated were Quisling appointees, and they were "ordained" by other Quisling-named bishops who themselves had never been ordained. This was in sharp conflict with Church statutes and traditions.

The Christian Council's reply further pointed out that the plan for placing Bishop Berggrav "on another level than that of the other bishops" made further negotiations impossible. In conclusion, however, the Christian Council declared that it was willing to take up negotiations with the Department "on the condition that all our bishops, with Berggrav at the head, participate in them."

Nazi Pressure Tactics Persist

However, not all the Nazis' "Church activities" during the months of April, May, and June were devoted to effecting a reconciliation. Every once in a while they would cast aside their peace-maker's mask and reveal their true selves, and their true intents and purposes.

After his release from Grini concentration camp on April 15th, Bishop Eivind Berggrav was placed under "house arrest." That is to say, he was confined to a small cottage in Asker and kept constantly under heavy police guard. As this is being written, Bishop Berggrav is still thus confined. The eleven police officers who guard the cottage day and night are equipped with helmets, rifles, revolvers, and clubs. The Bishop is never allowed to leave the premises and he is denied all communication with the outside world. With him for many months was his son, Öyvind, but the two were never permitted to see each other. Nor is the Bishop permitted to see his wife who has been confined to her bed elsewhere by illness.

In May it was reported that Bishop Wollert Krohn-Hansen, of Tromsö, had been arrested and placed in Lanes concentration camp.

About the same time came word that the Nazis had confiscated all property belonging to Bishop Henrik Hille. It was also learned that Dean Arne Fjellbu, of Trondheim Cathedral, was—like Berggrav—being held under "house arrest" somewhere in Tröndelag.

Nazi dismissals of non-Nazi pastors continued, and by mid-May the total had reached forty-five. Many of these were denied the right to speak in public. Late in May the Royal Norwegian Government in London learned the names of five Norwegian pastors who were still under arrest, despite recent Nazi assurances to the Norwegian people that churchmen were not to be arrested and imprisoned.

On Pentecost Sunday, May 24th, police entered Röa Church near Oslo and arrested Pastor Riise Hansen just as he was entering the sacristy. The service was suspended and the congregation sent home. The minister, wearing full vestments, was taken away in a police patrol and was held under "house arrest" for several days before being released. On the same Sunday a number of other pastors were brought to police headquarters for questioning. One pastor, prohibited from preaching in his own church, posted a notice on the door that the service would be held a half hour later than the usual time at another place. And so it was. Apparently the police did not dare interfere.

Quisling Bishops "Ordained"

Perhaps the most brazen of the Nazis' anti-Church acts during these early summer months was the "ordination" of two Quisling-appointed bishops at Our Savior's church in Oslo on Sunday, June 28th. The ceremony, witnessed by Quisling and other high Nazis, saw Lars Fröyland "ordained" as Bishop of Oslo, and Ludvig Daae Zwilgmeyer as Bishop of Skien. Officiating was the Quisling-named Bishop of Nidaros, Einar Lothe, who was assisted by four other Nazi bishops: Kvasnes of Stavanger, Hansen of Hamar, Sivertsen of Hammerfest and Dagfinn Zwilgmeyer of Bergen. None of these has ever been properly ordained. The text for the day was: "He sat upon the throne and said: Behold, I make all things new."

In the ordination sermon "Dean" Hagen, of Oslo, de-

clared the Church must endeavor to "win back" the youth
and the laboring masses. He congratulated the "bishops"
for having volunteered to fight "for the New Day over
Norway and for Norwegian Christian life." Later in the
ceremony, "Bishop" Fröyland declared that harshness was
often for the good of the individual concerned. "It is often
necessary," he declared, "for the Church to make intrusions which are for the good of the patient. One must
retaliate when attacked. Christ's words about love do not
mean that one should not defend oneself."

The "ordinations" did not come as a surprise. On the
Sunday before the ceremony a significant statement was
read from the pulpit of Our Savior's Church where the
event later took place. This declared that none of the three
permanent pastors of the church would assist in the ceremony, and that neither the organist nor others of the
church staff would be present. State police had to intervene
in order to assure that the church would be available for
the ceremony. For several days the police were unable to
obtain the keys for the church. Finally, late in the evening
before the ceremony, they found them hidden in the
home of one of the church wardens who had refused to
surrender them. The organ was also locked, and the Nazis
did not succeed in opening it until just as the service was
to begin.

"Ordinations" Protested

On the same Sunday that these two "ordinations" took
place, a sharp protest against them was read in almost all
other Norwegian churches.

It pointed out that the ordinations could not be considered to have taken place according to Church law and the Word of God, and further emphasized that the Norwegian Service Book states that bishops shall be inaugurated by other bishops. Thus, since all of Norway's properly ordained bishops have resigned, the "ordinations" were in conflict with the old, established tradition of the Norwegian Church. The protest warned that the June 28th events "were only beginning," and it urged the public to support the fighting Norwegian Church with prayers.

To Lars Fröyland, would-be successor to Eivind Berggrav as Bishop of Oslo, the deans and pastors of the diocese sent the following letter: "Among all the blows suffered by our Norwegian Church there is scarcely any which pastors and congregations have viewed with greater pain than the fact that you, 'Pastor' Fröyland, supported by the present government, allowed yourself to be appointed as bishop. Since news of this appointment and even about your ordination has been published in the newspapers, we take it for granted that it actually is your intention and that of the government to force upon pastors and congregations of the diocese a new bishop, despite the procedure laid down by existing Church statutes. It cannot possibly be unknown to you that pastors and congregations in Oslo Diocese emphatically maintain that Dr. Eivind Berggrav is the rightful bishop."

In conclusion the letter forcibly criticized Fröyland's position and branded him a traitor.

The New Status of Pastors

Only 60 of Norway's approximately 1,000 pastors have maintained connection with the Quisling government. The others have severed all relations with the State. They no longer receive their salaries, which previously were paid by the State. All communications sent to them by the Department of Church and Education are returned unopened. They continue to minister to the spiritual needs of their congregations, holding that those duties were imposed on them by God through ordination. On the other hand, they have discontinued the various State-imposed duties, such as officiating at marriages. If, after a civil ceremony, a newly-married couple desires the blessing of the Church, the pastors gladly bestow this. They continue to perform baptisms, conduct confirmations, administer the sacraments, preach the Gospel, and officiate at funerals.

All State-granted titles have also been abandoned by the clergy, and they are now addressed merely as "Mr." or "Pastor." They have been adamant in their stand that all Church property, including houses of worship and parsonages, are in fact the property of the "Church in the people" and not of the State.

The Clergy Is Given Wide Support

Throughout their long struggle with the Nazis, the bishops, deans, and pastors of the State Church have constantly been ardently supported not only by the rank-and-file of membership in the State Church, but by the various "free," or non-State, Church and religious organizations.

From these sources letters, protests, appeals, and resolutions have flooded the Department of Church and Education.

Among the latest indications of this united sentiment against Nazi interference with the Church is a "pro memoria" sent to the Department by the combined "Theological" and "Congregational" faculties, which represent the "liberal" and "orthodox" lines of thought, respectively, in the State Church. It unconditionally defends the bishops and pastors in their stand against Nazism. Excerpt:

> Our Church's theological professors are by law designated as expert advisors for the Department of Church and Education as well as for the bishops in all theological or churchly matters. We recognize it as our duty to present this *pro memoria,* which simultaneously is being sent to all pastors of the country. The Evangelical Lutheran church draws a sharp line between religion and politics. The Church is not the lord of the State, nor a state within a state, but the State's conscience. . . . We cannot find that the statement, "The Foundations of the Church," (which was read from pulpits on April 5th) has in any way a political character and much less that it is any anti-State or rebellious action. We must, on the other hand, declare that it is what it presents itself as being, a confession and a statement wherein the pastors take their stand with regard to the religious and moral aspects of events which have recently occurred in our society. . . . To thus act the pastors have not only a right but a duty. The pastors are duty-bound to obey God's Word without respect to persons and without taking into consideration extraneous factors of political or other character.

The memorandum further states that the bishops were obliged to make their protest against the youth service plan since it was irreconcilable with the parents' and Church's

right and responsibility with respect to the spiritual upbringing of the children. Likewise, it states, the Church
had to let its voice be heard in connection with the pressure and treatment to which the nation's teachers were exposed. With regard to the imprisonment, dismissal and
the placing of other restrictions on pastors, the memorandum refers to the Biblical admonition that "one should
obey God more than man." It continues:

Regarding the depriving of pastors of the right and authority to preach the Gospel and administer the sacraments which
they received from the Church upon ordination, there is this
to be said: It is only the Church which through operation of
its ecclesiastical agencies can take back that which it through
ecclesiastical action has given. . . . The pastors' resignations
are not an act of sabotage. This is revealed by the fact that the
pastors are still performing their fundamental services as ministers and wish to continue doing so. The resignations are, on
the other hand, a declaration of the Church's freedom and independence in spiritual matters. The Church has a right to
demand that this freedom and independence be respected by
the government of the State.

In May the Department of Church and Education also
received a protest from nineteen "free" religious organizations which declared:

The undersigned cannot remain silent in view of the manner
in which the State powers have branded the men of the Church
in connection with the statement which was read in the
churches at Easter. If the Church's pastors are to be denied the
right to set up the Church's profession of faith and to read it
to their congregations, and to act according to it without being
accused of politics, treason and rebellion, then it will be considered by the Christian people of Norway that the persecution

of Christianity has already begun here in our country. We express our complete agreement with the statement, "The Foundations of the Church," and place ourselves solidly behind our pastors.

Nor can we remain silent in view of the treatment to which the teachers have been subjected by the authorities. To force the teachers to enter into something which conflicts with their convictions and to subject them to terrible treatment if they refuse, is more revolting to us than we can say. Together with the clergy of Tröndelag, we ask mercy for these suffering people in the name of Jesus Christ.

Nor can we remain silent in view of the treatment of Bishop Berggrav. The action of the Department of Justice in sending reports to the foreign press that Berggrav has been released while simultaneously interning him so strictly that not even his own family is allowed to visit him, is not only dishonorable, but is also dishonest.

The nineteen groups signing this protest included various youth and mission organizations, the Deaconess' Association, the Council of Dissenters, the Norwegian Lutheran Free Church and the Seventh Day Adventist Congregation of Oslo.

Bishop John Mangers of the Catholic Church in Norway made his attitude known immediately after Berggrav and his colleagues lodged their initial protest of February 14th. Bishop Mangers sent a message stating he was in full agreement with the stand taken by the bishops and with the course they had pursued.

The Nazis May Widen Attack

Whether the Nazis will widen their attack on the Norwegian State Church to include the "free" religious organizations in Norway still remains to be seen. An indication that such plans may be in the making appeared in mid-July when the Quisling-controlled press reported that the Norwegian foreign missions would in all likelihood be liquidated and a "new arrangement" made for all missionary activity. The old system of sending money from Norway to distant parts of the globe was sharply criticized, and it was brought out that the Norwegian foreign missions formerly used to send 1,800,000 kroner annually to the mission fields.

"So long as we remain a poor people," said the Quisling press, "we have no right to send money out of the country. Those countries, which in this way benefit by Norwegian generosity, are not under Norwegian sovereignty, and by making gifts to them we help the various nations economize on their colonial budgets."

It is a well-known fact that the various mission organizations in Norway have a combined capital of several million kroner, and it is feared that these moneys will be seized by Nasjonal Samling, Quisling's party.

CHAPTER X

THE CHURCH—FEARLESS AND
UNSHAKABLE

As a motto for the Norwegian Church's fight against Nazism might be used the words of Jesus: "Fear not those who destroy the body, but are not able to destroy the soul, but rather fear him who is able to destroy both the body and the soul." Under the tremendous risk of having its outward ecclesiastical organization smashed to pieces and its true servants persecuted and terrorized by a physically superior and pagan power, the Church has stood fearless and unshakable. It has not yielded an inch in the fight for its soul, for its religious freedom, for its Christian foundation of faith, and in a wider sense for the foundation of justice upon which Norway's Christian civilization has been built. With open eyes the Norwegian Church has, in an historic time, taken the same position as that assumed by Luther at Worms when he spoke those definitive words: "Here I stand. I cannot do otherwise. So help me God. Amen."

The Church has been through a process of purification and has merged more closely than ever before with the Norwegian people. The miraculous welding together of the united Christian front is one of the great results. Another is the religious awakening which has spread over Norway in the midst of all its hardship.

Bishop Berggrav gave expression to this in a greeting sent to the Swedish Church assembly in May, 1941. "God has led the Norwegian Christians into the great melting pot," he wrote, "where everything belonging to us has become small, and God has become great." Norway's chair at that assembly remained vacant because the Nazi authorities had refused the Church permission to send representatives.

Out of this melting pot rose also Dr. Kristian Schelderup, theologian and scientist, former spokesman of a strongly critical religious liberalism, and founder of a school of humanism in Norway. It caused widespread interest and joy when this socially-alert and searching man stood forth and confessed his return to a living, positive Christianity. This was in reality more than a private affair. It was the first sign of a spiritual trend which had been freed of its slag and dross and melted into pure metal. Dr. Schelderup had at last found the full expression for his rich personality and had become a living force in the Church. On his travels about the country, large crowds assembled everywhere to hear him speak. At one such meeting, held in a Bergen church during the critical October days of 1941, he expressed the prevailing spirit of the Church front when he said: "Christianity was born in sufferings, in prisons and in death, and that is why the Cross became its symbol. How is it with us and our Christian sincerity? Can *we* sacrifice? The day may be nearer than anyone believes, when it will again mean risking your life to confess your complete adherence to Christ's name."

None of the listeners were in doubt as to who the speaker meant as the source of the threatening danger. Nor was the local Nazi press leader in doubt. A few days after the meeting, in an article published in one of the local Nazi-controlled newspapers, he called upon Dr. Schelderup to "confirm" that this statement was not intended to imply any danger from Germany, but from Russia. Naturally, no such confirmation was forthcoming.

But after February 1, 1942, the danger of martyrdom for the Church and its leaders swept in from a direction whence all had expected it, and the Church has lost none of its courageous willingness to choose, if necessary, the way of the Cross. It has become an example for the entire world, and—best of all—an inspiration to the Norwegian people in their fight against evil powers for the cause of justice and freedom.

The following words, taken from a handbill secretly distributed during the Church's greatest crisis, reflect this inspiration and express the people's gratitude to the Church:

The Norwegian people today look up to their Church's leaders, and thank them for their unyielding stand and their faithful watch over sacred trusts, and unitedly the people will stand behind them in the fight which is now to be fought for truth and justice.

Because it will be a fight. A fight between two cultures, Christian and barbarian—a fight *for* everything we love and hold dear, and *against* the rule of brutality and injustice. Because who can stop the Norwegian people when they unitedly go to battle for our faith, our culture, our children and for the *future*? For nearly two years we have been fighting hard. But we have been forced to remain on the defensive. *Now we are shifting from defense to attack!*

. . . Finally, let us—this time—make it clear: The Norwegian people are on the march. It is the duty of every single Norwegian to join in. We have leaders who might stir the envy of anyone. We will follow them, cost what it may. The Norwegian Church's fight is Norway's fight. Because the Church is the common home of all of us. And it houses all our prized possessions. The fight shall be fought in the catacombs. From now on the light shall come from the Church. Tyranny shall be fought to defeat. Soon will come the time when we shall emerge from our shelters and build our country in the way it must and shall be built.

Spring is coming!

CHAPTER XI

THE ESTABLISHMENT OF A "FREE" CHURCH CONFIRMED

The deduction that the Church of Norway had severed relations with the State and had set itself up as a "free" Church was confirmed in July, 1942, when six prominent churchmen, acting as a "temporary leadership of the Church," issued a manifesto which emphasized that, regardless of dismissals and other encroachments by the State, the Church would henceforth carry on independently of the present government.

The six men comprising the Church's "temporary leadership" are Bishops Henrick Hille and James Maroni, Dean Johannes Hygen, Professor Ole C. Hallesby, the Rev. H. E. Wislöff and Ludvig Hope, a noted evangelist and writer on religious subjects. Dean Hygen is acting as the representative of Bishop Eivind Berggrav, of Oslo, who is still being held under "house arrest."

The manifesto was sent to all pastors and congregational councils of the church and was read to congregations on Sunday, July 26th. It reviewed the long series of events leading up to the final breach, the present situation of the Church, and outlined the goals towards which the Church is fighting. Finally, it urged pastors and congregational councils, regardless of any governmental interference, to continue their proper functions in collaboration with the rightful bishops of the Church.

"These things," declared the *New York Times* in an editorial, "were said in the very presence of death. There can be no one of any religion, who acknowledges a moral law in the universe, who will not take off his hat in reverence to these brave men."

Apparently the Nazis were confused as to how to deal with this new development. Quisling waited several weeks before making any public acknowledgment of it. Then, after consulting with his Minister of Church and Education and his Minister of Domestic Affairs, he stepped forward in mid-August and announced that the "temporary Church leadership" was to be considered dissolved. But his words did not suffice to accomplish the fact. The leadership still stands, and under it the Church of Norway is functioning smoothly once again.

How long this situation will last is a question only time itself will answer. . . .

Following is the complete text of the manifesto as issued by the present church leadership:

A Declaration of Church Policy

"Inasmuch as we have assumed the highly responsible task of standing as the supreme leadership for our Church in the present situation, we find it necessary to supply an orientation of the reasons for the break between the present State Church authorities and the Church, of the aims of the fight which the Church has been forced to carry on, and of the work remaining before us.

I. *The Church's Fight*

"In the summer of 1940 Reichskommissar Terboven promised the Church full freedom on the condition that it refrained from political activity.

"The Church retained this freedom as long as the Administrative Council functioned.

"But after September 25th of the same year this situation immediately changed. It became clear that those men who assumed the power held a view on the relationship between State and Church which conflicts with the view expressed in our Church's confession, and on which our State Church arrangement is based. (We here refer to the interpretation in "The Church's Order" and "The Foundations of the Church.")

"The State wished to rule the Church and to make the Church its servant. In the broadcasting of religious services we saw the situation become so impossible that the Church's consultant was forced to resign from his duties, and most preachers found that they could not longer participate in such broadcasts. We mention also the ungracious reception of the bishops' protest against the Hird's brutal attacks in the schools, which the Department of Church and Education had observed without taking steps to bring the assailants to account. The ministers' pledge of silence was discontinued in conflict with the ancient and commonly accepted ecclesiastical rule which both obligates the pastor and guarantees his right to remain silent about that which is confided to him in his ministry. The authorization of Feyling's textbook is also a typical example. Here politics are introduced into the teaching of Christianity in the children's schools. The book was also authorized illegally, inasmuch as the legally-prescribed advisors were not consulted.

"Clear proof that the State wanted to force the Church to take a stand in favor of a certain political philosophy was the practice which the Department employed in the making of official appointments. In one letter the Department declared the pastors' attitude towards the New Order would determine whether they were to be appointed to offices in the Church. Following the same direction was another letter from the Department stating that in instances where the Church and organizations accept Nasjonal Samling and the New Order no obstacles would be placed in the path of religious work. The Department of Church and Education also wanted to reserve for itself the right to define the preaching of God's Word; in a letter it submitted directives to the effect that the pastors should preach the edifying and eternal aspects of the Gospel and not touch upon the problems of the day. In this connection we must also mention the decree regarding compulsory youth service, a means of rearing children independently of the home and Church and in conflict with most parents' convictions as well as with the Church and school laws.

"The authorities also resorted to the use of force against the Church and its men. The Bishop's pastoral letter of 1941 was confiscated by the police who forbade pastors from reading it to their congregations. On February 1st of this year the Department arranged a political worship in the Trondheim Cathedral and then dismissed Dean Fjellbu because he on the same day, but at another hour, conducted the regular devotions for his congregation while the police, through the use of force, prevented the people of the congregation from entering their own church.

"In connection with these and a long series of other encroachments, which not only violated the Church's legal rights but also its inner spiritual life and the freedom of conscience, the men of the Church drew up a confession which was entitled "The Foundations of the Church." This expresses, simply and clearly, the Church's God-given right to freedom in relation to worldly power. But when this confession was read in the churches, the men responsible for it were arrested. Even before this happened all the bishops had been dismissed. Up to that time the Church, through its bishops and pastors, had been content to protest in words. But now when it had been proved abundantly that words had no effect on the authorities, the Church was forced to take action. Therein lies the reason for the resignations, first the bishops' on February 24th and later the deans' and pastors', from Easter and on. There was no single act by the State against the Church (e.g., the Trondheim affair) which was the reason for these resignations, but the conflict of principles in the State's and the Church's views which became more and more clear. The two theological faculties declared in a statement of April 24th of this year that when the State resorts to such encroachments and violations of law against the Church, it constitutes a breach of our State Church constitution. It therefore became necessary for the Church to free itself from its relationship to the present government. Inasmuch as it was declared simultaneously with the resignations that those concerned would continue to perform their duties to the extent it was possible for a non-official to do so, it will be noted that the purpose of the action was neither to strike nor to commit sabotage.

"Not only did the State encroach upon the administration of the Church, its time-honored orderliness and legal right, but even upon the performance of ministerial duties. There were issued injunctions against speaking in public, injunctions against wearing of clerical robes and against use of titles. People were sent to a number of churches to control the pastors' sermons. Pastors were reported for sermons, and a number of pastors were arbitrarily dismissed. Since, as mentioned above, one must meet the condition of joining a political movement before being given a position in the Church, there arose a shortage of pastors to fill the vacant posts, despite the fact that there were available a number of young men who had fully completed their education for the ministry. To make up for this shortage the authorities seized upon the solution of appointing and ordaining as pastors certain laymen who lacked the most essential prerequisites for the ministry. It has made an especially strong impression that new bishops have been appointed in conflict with the Altar Book, which contains the applicable Norwegian law. Nor can we refrain from mentioning the revoltingly strict confinement of Bishop Berggrav.

"It is not with joy that the Church has taken the serious step of severing connections with the State.

"But it had to do it.

"It was at the behest of conscience and after serious consideration that it occurred. The Church would not have been faithful to its Master if it had calmly allowed all this to happen without taking action.

"II. The Situation Today

"It might seem that the Church has suffered a defeat. The Church posseses no instruments of force, nor does it wish to employ such instruments.

"But in reality the Church has won a spiritual victory.

"During the very days of the Easter season, and immediately thereafter, when the men of the Church were being subjected to police hearings, dismissals, prohibition of speech, arrests, confiscation of property, threats of deportation and even of the death penalty—precisely at that time it was established that the Church could not be frightened; it continued to preach openly God's Word and gospel, and as the conscience of the State it continued to protest against the encroachments which the authorities had made upon the Church, the schools, the parents and children—in short, on the country's established legal system.

"Voluntarily it submitted to the sacrifices and sufferings imposed upon it. Voluntarily it surrendered the salaries which its servants previously had received through the State from ecclesiastical funds and property.

"The Church's victory was that when the test came it actually obeyed God more than man.

"This is the Church's inner and spiritual victory.

"But outwardly the victory was also great.

"Our Church has 738 pastors in office. Of these more than 90 per cent have resigned, and others are steadily joining them. The congregational councils have solidly supported their pastors.

"The authorities have made several efforts to negotiate. We, on our side, have informed the Department that we were ready at any time to enter into negotiations, but only on the condition that our bishops, with Berggrav at the head, participate on behalf of the Church. This demand of ours is a consequence of our declaration that the dismissed bishops are the rightful bishops of the Church.

"III. The Aims of the Battle

"For the first: The goal is not of political nature. We are loyal to the occupying power within the limits set down by international law. The fight which we have been forced to take up against the present government's encroachments on Church, schools, parents, children, the certainty of justic, and the freedom of conscience, is not politically motivated.

"For the second: The goal is not of ecclesiastical-political nature. To be sure, there are some who contend that we should now enter upon a reorganization of our Church. But if we think this matter through, it becomes clear for us that it is not advisable to embark on this project just now. While the Church fights its fight of life or death, it is necessary that we stand together as one man and therefore avoid questions difficult to discuss.

"For the third: The goal is of a spiritual nature. We

have not taken up this fight in order to destroy the State Church, nor for the purpose of establishing a free people's Church or free Church. On the whole, we are not fighting for a Church readjustment. We are fighting for the Church, for the Church's innermost being and most precious right, for its God-given mission of preaching God's Word and of living its especial life in the midst of the State. We fight this battle so that the Church we have can perform the duty which is the duty of the Church, namely to minister to the congregations with words and sacraments. Therefore we declared that the bishops and pastors, no matter whether they were dismissed or resigned from office, are our rightful bishops and pastors, who shall continue their ministry regardless of the changed relations to the State. Therefore we do not wish to break with anything more in our Church's arrangement than is absolutely necessary in order that the Church might perform its duties.

"Briefly, we can state as follows: We fight this battle so that we may work free and unrestrained. Unrestrained outwardly by the State's illegal encroachments, and free inwardly with a clear conscience before the Church's Master and His Sacred Word.

"IV. Our Tasks

"Therewith new light is thrown on our responsibilities and duties.

"We shall not bide our time waiting for sensational events in the Church conflict, nor shall we waste this critical time in planning the reorganization of the Church.

"No, we shall work and make use of the freedom to work which our fight has given us. We shall work in our Church. We shall work within the system and those institutions our Church now has. In this time of crisis we do not wish to break away from anything in our Church other than its relationship to a government which, because of its stand with respect to the Church, has made the breach necessary.

"It was perhaps natural that some time had to pass after the resignations before the work of the Church was again resumed under the new conditions. But now the time is here when we as a united flock must devote ourselves to the full work of the Church:

"A. The congregational councils will continue their duties no matter whether they are dismissed or not, seeing to it that all the Church work in the congregations proceeds on schedule. They will be in contact with the rightful deans and bishops. Pastors who are members of congregational councils will continue in the councils even though they have resigned office or have been dismissed.

"B. The pastors will continue their ministry in the congregations even though they have resigned office or have been dismissed. As long as the Church has not deprived them of that duty which they accepted upon ordination, they have the right to wear clerical robes and to perform those services in the Church which a non-official can perform. In all ministerial matters they are to consult their superiors, the rightful deans and bishops.

"C. The deans will continue their regular duties in connection with their rightful bishops.

"D. The bishops will direct the Church work within their respective dioceses by continuing to hold their offices as bishops, conducting visitations and ordinations, and, on the whole, by continuing their customary duties. They have the full of authority of the Church to wear the robes of bishops and to use the title of bishop.

"E. Since there now is established a Church leadership, which will deal with matters concerning the whole Church, our Church has its entire working apparatus in operation. It is up to us whether the work is to be done or not. Every single one of us, with faith in God and with loyalty to our Church's Master, must now perform the duty which He has entrusted to us. Let us use the available time to work while it is still day. Today we stand before an open door with vast possibilities. The Lord grant us all humility, faith and obedience enough to enter upon those tasks which He has prepared for us. Assuredly all of us have felt that we in this time have been under the mighty hand of God. Through the punishment which has befallen our people and the entire world we have heard God's voice. But we have been permitted to learn that God is merciful even while He punishes. When we now look back over these past two years, we discover with sacred wonder and adoration, the numerous blessings which have been poured out upon our Church and our people. In truth, the Lord has placed before us an open door: The people are seeking out God's House as never before in our generation. Consciences are open to the truth. Every alert preacher can rejoice over the new interest in hearing God's message. From all parts of our far-flung country come reports of many great revivals—quiet, wholesome, deep-seated revivals. God has in mercy visited our people. Let us thank God and pray that He in mercy will direct His work forward to a nationwide revival so that our people also may emerge from this ordeal by fire as a new and cleansed people. Groups of our people who have stood far removed from the Church and Christianity are also beginning to discover the Church. They respect the Church and are beginning to look to it for guidance. Here also we see the Finger of God, and we thank Him for His mercy.

"We greet our pastors, congregational councils and the congregations and we thank you for your sincere contributions for unity and solidarity in this time of crisis. We understand that especially in out-of-the-way sections, where information is difficult to obtain and often delayed, the strain has been especially acute. With faith in our Heavenly Father we dare to look to the future with confidence and good cheer. In the words of the old psalmist: 'My soul waiteth in silence for God only.' "

Oslo, July 1, 1942.

O. HALLESBY
JOHS. HYGEN
HENRIK HILLE
J. MARONI
LUDVIG HOPE
H. E. WISLÖFF

CHAPTER XII

THE CHURCH CARRIES ON

MEMBERS OF THE Temporary Church Leadership remained in Oslo for several weeks following issuance of the manifesto *freeing* the Norwegian Church of its traditional bonds with the State. Their chief reason for so doing became clear on September 12th when members of the group sent a letter to the Quisling Department of Church and Education stating that there could be no question of opening negotiations as long as the Nazi officials demanded an advance declaration obligating the Church to recognize the Quisling government.

It was then ascertained that throughout a major potion of the intervening weeks the Quisling authorities had been "trying" to get negotiations started, and that the leaders had been standing by to await developments. Eventually, however, it became evident that the Nazis' overtures were not seriously intended. Their real purpose was either to trick the Leadership into making a statement that could be interpreted as rebellious and thereby justify arrests and other acts of violence, or else—by proffering the release of Bishop Berggrav—to lure the Leadership into making a statement which later could be held up before the Norwegian people as a political recognition of Quisling by the Church. At any rate, the Temporary Church Leadership was not to be trapped.

Report of the Temporary Church Leadership

On September 14th the Leadership issued a notable report wherein it conscientiously accounted for all its activities during the weeks that had passed since its establishment. In connection with the proposed negotiations, this document emphasized that the Church had consistently taken the stand summarized by the following three points:

1. All negotiations must be conducted through the bishops of the Church, including Bishop Berggrav.
2. Bishop Berggrav must therefore be set free before negotiations commence. The entire Christian population of Norway is deeply shocked by the treatment to which Bishop Berggrav has been subjected and regards the hardship imposed on him as an attack on the Church.
3. All negotiations must be conducted on a free and open basis without advance conditions.

The report then reviewed in detail the various attempts that had been made to open negotiations ever since June 12th. It told of how the Quisling Department of Domestic Affairs had arbitrarily "dissolved" the Temporary Church Leadership shortly after its formation in July. To this the bishops had replied that "in view of the Church's actual position today and in view of our own responsibility as to its future, we cannot revoke appointment of the Temporary Church Leadership." The Nazis backed down, and soon they were making direct overtures to members of the Leadership, especially to Professor O. Hallesby and Dean Johannes Hygen.

According to the report, efforts to arrange negotiations had stranded again and again on the Nazis' failure to extract from the Church leaders various advance statements which they were not disposed to make. Finally, on September 12th, the bishops had notified the Department of Church and Education that on the basis of all letters received from this office it appeared more important to obtain the advance statement than to get the negotiations themselves under way. "If the government regards this point as the real kernel of the negotiations," wrote the bishops, "then it is an unreasonable demand that this should be decided in advance and before the negotiations get started. And it is still more unreasonable that an imprisoned bishop should be expected to take a stand on this vital point. We therefore wish to state that if the government insists on an advance statement there is no possibility of opening negotiations. On this point we cannot waver."

However, the bishops reiterated their willingness to open negotiations on the conditions originally laid down by them and listed above.

The Temporary Church Leadership's report of September 14th concluded as follows:

Here we stand today. God has given us grace to stand up under all this with boldness, and we have felt ourselves borne by the confidence and prayers of pastors and congregations. We do not know now whether there will be negotiations or a breach, but here, too, we stand boldly. Let us all carry on, according to our old purpose, in calm and composure, and let us all stand together in prayer for our Church and our people in this critical time. We hold firmly to the Lord's promise: "To them that love God, all things work together for good."

The report was signed by Bishops Maroni, Fleischer, Hille, Skagestad, and Krohn-Hansen; also by Professor Hallesby, Dean Hygen and the Rev. H. E. Wislöff.

On the very day the report was issued, the Quisling Department of Church and Education sent out a statement, in the form of a "White Book," signed by Ragnar Skancke and Sigmund Feyling. In it they declared that the authorities could not open negotiations "until the former bishops resign all political activity and openly recognize Quisling."

Other Events of Summer and Fall

In the final analysis, the futile efforts to get negotiations started, extending from June into September, formed merely a pale and almost ironical background for other incidents rising out of the church conflict during this period. Many of these, to be sure, were of only passing interest, but taken together they reflect unmistakably not only the Nazis' real attitude towards the Church but also their frustration in coping with it.

Late in June the printing of Bibles was discontinued in Norway when Reichkommissar Terboven prohibited the sale of paper for that purpose. . . . A few days after the "ordination" of the new Nazi Bishop of Oslo,[1] the people were given a glimpse of the type of men who

[1] See page 114.

were responding to the Nazis' appeals for pastors to fill the pulpits of men who had been dismissed. "Ordained" in a moving-picture-studio atmosphere of floodlights and cameras at Our Savior's Church in Oslo were a former distributor of religious tracts named Barby, alias Olsen, and a notorious religious fanatic named Rabben who had been discharged from his position as traveling representative for the Santal Mission because of embezzlement. . . . In August the Quisling Department of Church and Education ordered police to confiscate clerical robes belonging to pastors who ventured to wear them in accordance with the instructions given by the Temporary Church Leadership in its July manifesto. . . . Occasionally came reports of pastors being arrested. . . . Efforts were reported made at various places to obstruct funerals being conducted by pastors who had been "dismissed" by the Nazis. . . . The Gestapo ransacked the home of the pastor at Trysil. . . . "Dismissed" pastors were questioned as to how they were obtaining means to exist (the answer was always the same: anonymous donors). . . . All but one of the deans were "dismissed" and Dean Hygen was ordered to move from Oslo. . . . Two noted pastors, H. E. Wislöff and Ingvald B. Carlsen were similarly banished. . . . Dr. Kristian Schelderup [2] of Bergen was arrested. . . . The Nazi "Bishop," Lars Fröyland, attempting to conduct visitations in Oslo, found himself refused admittance at parsonage after parsonage; finally he had to call upon police to help him.

In August Vidkun Quisling spent a vacation in his

2 See page 123.

native village of Fyresdal and while there paid a visit to
the home of the local pastor, the Rev. Otto Irgens. Quisling arrived at the parsonage with a full escort of cars
and police officers. He remained several hours, questioning the pastor and upbraiding the clergy in general. Now
and then the Norwegian führer would fly into a rage,
calling the Norwegian clergy, a "gang of criminals," or
assuring Irgens that the only reason he (Irgens) had not
been shot was "consideration for his family—no, consideration for the village where the Quisling family had
resided for 400 years!" In a final explosion Quisling declared Irgens "dismissed" and said that everything he
owned was to be taken from him. On Quisling's orders
the police then proceeded to strip the parsonage bare,
and they did a thorough job of it. They even took the
preserves from the cellar and the loose change from the
pastor's pocketbook. As for clothes, the pastor and his
wife were allowed to retain only those they happened to
be wearing.

And despite all this there were times when threats
against the Church or clergy were "hushed up" almost
the moment after they had been made. This was generally
attributed to interference by the German authorities who,
it was said, desired to see the Church conflict subside.
Yet, on the other hand, many actions against the Church
and clergy, although carried out by Quisling adherents,
were directly traceable to the Germans. This confusion,
whether intentional or not, has been a constant factor in
the Norwegian church conflict.

The Nazis Issue An Appeal

A month after hope for negotiations had been openly abandoned by both sides in the conflict, the Quisling Department of Church and Education sent out a circular letter to all clergymen. Dated October 15th, it appealed for "a better understanding of official church policy," and listed a number of new regulations regarding clergymen's salaries and clergymen's duties in community affairs.

The pastors were curtly informed that those of them who had failed to draw their State salaries for the final quarter of the 1941–42 fiscal year (April-June) would have to regard these as "lost." Those who had not drawn salaries for the first quarter of the new fiscal year were given until November 1 to do so, otherwise these moneys would also revert "to the benefit of the State." These rules applied to the overwhelming majority of Norwegian clergymen, since virtually all of them had resigned from their "official" positions the previous spring and had from then on refused to accept compensation from the State.

The Department's letter went on to state that no one could understand better than the clergymen what had been lost for the Church through "its disconnection with public life." Admitting that "quite a great number of clergymen" have refused to function in their "official" capacity, the letter pointed out that the Department had been forced to arrange for civil registration of births and marriages. "Even through this," it continued, "the Church has lost possibilities of keeping in contact with the Norwegian people, and some of these possibilities unfortunately cannot be regained. The clergymen who are on strike have assumed a severe responsibility through their behavior the last six months."

"Each Stone a Challenge"

Needless to say, this Nazi appeal, with its mixture of warning and offer of bribes, went unheeded. The Church had set its course and clung to it. And it grew constantly stronger in the process. Each new blow directed at it served but to bring about a rededication of effort and a renewal of determination.

The Nazis continued their harassing tactics. Additional pastors were banished from their congregations and home communities. Police were ordered to see to it that the regular bishops did not leave their homes, thus preventing them from conducting visitations and ordinations. Several leading religious journals were ordered suspended by the Nazis, and in order to disrupt the contact between pastors and their congregations all parish papers were banned. To a constantly increasing degree the few pro-Nazi pastors served as spies on other clergymen, conveying their "tattle-tale" information to Quisling authorities. Thus an Oslo pastor was "reported" for having refused to shake hands with one of the new Nazi "bishops"; shortly afterwards he was banished from Oslo. Nazi police closed the headquarters of the "clerical opposition" and confiscated all files and documents belonging to the Temporary Church Leadership.

The Church Keeps on Fighting

If any evidence was needed to prove that the Church opposition to Nazism was not weakening under this treatment it came in November, 1942, when the Temporary Church Leadership, supported by many other religious groups of other denominations, sent directly to Minister President Quisling a sharp protest against the Jewish persecution which was then being carried on by the Nazis. It was the voice of the Norwegian Church speaking out once again, as fearless and forcible as ever before.

Not only the leaders of the Church took up this fight. On Sunday, November 15th, and again on Sunday, November 22nd, prayers were said in all Norwegian churches for the persecuted Jews. Once again the pastors and the people of Norway had lined up solidly behind the Church leaders.

Following is the text of the Temporary Church Leadership's protest against Jewish persecutions in Norway:

"To Minister President Quisling:

"The Minister President's law, announced October 27, 1942, regarding the confiscation of property belonging to Jews has been received by our people with great sorrow which was deepened by the decree that all Jewish men over 15 years of age were to be arrested.

"When we now appeal to the Minister President it is not to defend whatever wrongs Jews may have committed. If they have committed crimes they shall be tried, judged and punished according to Norwegian law, just as all other citizens. But those who have committed no crime shall enjoy the protection of our country's justice.

"For 91 years Jews have had a legal right to reside and earn a livelihood in our country. Now they are being deprived of their property without warning, and thereafter the men are being arrested and thus prevented from providing for their propertyless wives and children. This conflicts not only with the Christian commandment of 'love thy neighbor,' but with the most elemental of legal rights. These Jews have not been charged with any transgression of the country's laws, much less convicted of such transgressions by judicial procedure. Nevertheless they are being punished as severely as the worst criminals are punished. They are being punished because of their racial background, wholly and solely because they are Jews.

"This disaffirmation by the authorities of the Jews' worth as human beings is in sharp conflict with the Word of God which from cover to cover proclaims all racial groups to be of one blood. See particularly Acts 17:26. There are few points where God's Word speaks more plainly than here. God does not differentiate among people. Romans 2:11. There is neither Jew nor Greek. Galatians 3:28. There is no difference. Romans 3:22. Above all else: When God through incarnation became man, He allowed Himself to be born in a Jewish home of a Jewish mother.

"Thus, according to God's Word, all people have, in the first instance, the same human worth and thereby the same human rights. Our state authorities are by law obliged to respect this basic view. Paragraph 2 of the Constitution states that the Evangelical Lutheran religion will remain the religion of the State. That is to say, the State cannot enact any law or decree which is in conflict with the Christian faith or the Church's Confession.

"When we now appeal to the authorities in this matter we do so because of the deepest dictates of conscience. By remaining silent about this legalized injustice against the Jews we would make ourselves co-guilty in this injustice. If we are to be true to God's Word and to the Church's Confession we must speak out.

"Regarding worldly authority our Confession states that it has nothing to do with the soul but that it shall 'protect the bodies and corporal things against obvious injustice, and keep the people in check in order to maintain civic peace and order.' Augustana, Article 28. This corresponds with God's Word which says the authority is of God and established by him as 'not a terror to good works, but to the evil.' Romans 13:3.

"If the worldly authority becomes a terror to good works, that is, to the one who does not transgress against the country's laws, then it is the Church's God-given duty as the conscience of the State to object.

"The Church, namely, has God's call and full authority to proclaim God's law and God's gospel. Therefore it cannot remain silent when God's commandments are being trampled underfoot. And now it is one of Christianity's basic values which is violated; the commandments of God which are fundamental to all society, namely law and justice.

"Here one cannot dismiss the Church with a charge that it is mixing into politics. The apostles spoke courageously to the authorities of their day and said: 'We ought to obey God rather than men.' Acts 5:29. Luther says: 'The Church does not interfere in worldly matters when it warns the authority to be obedient to the highest authority, which is God.'

"By the right of this our calling we therefore warn our people to desist from injustice, violence and hatred. He who lives in hatred and encourages evil invokes God's judgment upon himself.

"The Minister President has on several occasions emphasized that Nasjonal Samling, according to its program, will safeguard the basic values of Christianity. Today one of these values is in danger. If it is to be protected, it must be protected soon.

"We have mentioned it before, but re-emphasize it now in closing: This appeal of ours has nothing to do with politics. Before worldly authority we maintain that obedience in all temporal matters which God's Word demands."

(Sixty signatures followed.)

The People of Norway

The courage and high purpose of the leaders of the Norwegian Church would have been of little avail in the fight against Nazism had they failed to retain the support of the people of Norway—the 98 or 99 per cent of the entire population who have repeatedly by word and act, throughout nearly three years of German occupation, shown their complete and uncompromising detestation of Hitler and Quisling and everything they stand for.

Crisis after crisis has found the people's loyalty to the Church and its leaders unshaken, just as their loyalty to King Haakon and to the Royal Norwegian Government, now in London, has never wavered. The people have not only remained loyal, but also grateful.

The people, too, have courage. They have stood up to the Nazis whenever their trades or professions, organizations or institutions have been under attack. They have stood up to the Nazis just as bravely whenever they have been singled out for individual treatment—for arrest, torture or execution.

The people have made the Church's fight *their* fight, and the Nazis have learned that in attacking the Church, or any of its representatives, they are in fact attacking the people of Norway. Therefore it may be well, in closing this book, to provide the reader with a glimpse of what the average Norwegian is thinking about today, and how he or she views the future.

Such a glimpse can be found in the following letter, successfully smuggled out of the country in the fall of 1942. It was written by a girl to her brother who had earlier escaped from Norway in order to join the Norwegian fighting forces in Great Britain. Her innermost feelings were given spontaneous expression as her mind overflowed with thoughts prevalent in occupied Norway:

"Well, I hope this letter gets across the frontier and reaches you safely. Things are quite tolerable here in

Norway. The schools have started again, and travel and the mail function almost normally.

"Oh, but our feelings! Nobody outside can realize them. Just think that the best of our youth is imprisoned; our men are sent to Germany and their property stolen! One should not talk about hidden Norway now. It has blossomed forth. In our schools, workshops, offices and shops—everywhere—the same question is always asked: 'Are you Norwegian?' Those who are not—that is, those who belong to Quisling's Nasjonal Samling—are given a bad time. A Nasjonal Samling member wrote a while ago: 'Help me with a little food. To be an idealist in Norway is not fun. My former friends will not greet me. The butcher gives me little meat, and the baker gives me burnt bread!' These are only small things of course.

"We face grim times. The teachers will probably be sent to Germany; the women teachers are going to work in the hospitals. But there is a saying among the people of Norway today: 'So that the many may live, I must be prepared to sacrifice all, yes, even life itself.' And in spite of all that we suffer, many a Norwegian youth says: 'Thanks for the roses in the road, thanks for the thorns between, thanks for this ladder to heaven, thanks for a safe and eternal home.' As our own country and our own home are unsafe, the peace of heaven comes remarkably close. And because of that we see a new Norway rising. It looks like the old one, but it is much richer. In it is a people cleansed new by suffering.

"You should see our youth! They clench their teeth and they bear unheard-of suffering. With a smile on their lips they stand up to the heaviest burdens. The Germans rage and threaten. But, as is often said, we have something to suffer for.

"The children, too, are fine. I attended a children's outing recently. They sang the songs of the homeland —yes, even the King's Song. They watched for the Germans, and when they approached changed over to popular ditties of the moment. We have altered the National Anthem a little; we now sing 'And from England Haakon spoke, spoke against Germany,' Oh, how we long for the days when we can again sing our songs, speak and write freely! Because there are so many spies we must be very careful. Necessity has taught us to be careful even of our own people. It is a terrible situation. Where will it end?

"The people hope that together with the national renaissance which sweeps over our country like a prairie fire, will also come a religious reawakening. There is one thing—we all pray. And many think that the religious reawakening has already started.

"We all wonder how things are with you; I always think about you. If only you knew how often I wish I could be with you . . . free, able to fight in the open. But we fight together with you; many, many of us. We will wait and be ready to do more when the time comes.

"Give my thanks to the voices in London which bring us the news. We will hang on here. But it is sad that so many must die. What a people the Norwegians are! And what a country! Let money and property disappear. We shall be able to build it all again. The victory shall be ours!"

APPENDIX

PASTORAL LETTER OF FEBRUARY, 1941 [1]

To Our Congregations from the Bishops of the Church of Norway

We gratefully acknowledge the fact that the Church and all Christian societies and organizations, generally speaking, have been able to carry on their spiritual work up to the present. But signs of a growing unrest and anxiety are nevertheless becoming more and more evident. *Can the Church sit quietly on the sidelines while the Commandments of God are being set aside and while many other events are taking place which dissolve law and order?* The Church is an organization whose great calling is to spread the Gospel and unite all believers in a way of life in accordance with the will of God. Outwardly the Church is a worldly organization, heavy with human shortcomings and suffering from the fact that we, who are the instruments of the Church, are sinful. Even so, our Lord has called such men to be His servants from the very days of the Apostles, and He has promised them the mercy and the power by which He Himself leads His children.

The Christian congregation have their roots in a living spiritual communion founded by Jesus Christ, who is their Lord and Savior. The Church, therefore, belongs to God and must fulfill its mission freely and fearlessly, because God's word and God's will are above all else in this world.

The mission of the Church is identified with the very life of

[1] Published by the Royal Norwegian Government's Press Representatives in the U. S. A., Washington, D. C.

the people and is charged with complete responsibility for spreading His words of salvation based on the law of God.

The bishops of the Church of Norway, guided by their consciences and spurred on by the lack of clarity which surrounds them, see it as their clear duty to appeal to the authorities which today govern the life of the Church and the State.

After having consulted other Christians, the bishops on January 15, 1941, addressed a documented petition to the acting Head of the Department of Church and Education as follows:

"To the head of the department of Church and Education, Acting Secretary Skancke:

"The very foundation of the Church of Norway rests on a definite constitutional relationship to the State, and on the assumption that the duty of the State and all departments of the government is to uphold righteousness and justice in accordance with the will of God. The Norwegian Constitution states: 'The Evangelical Lutheran religion shall be the official religion of Norway.' It therefore is imperative and essential that the Church should know clearly whether the State, which is also concerned with ecclesiastical matters, accepts and honors the legal and moral obligations contained in the Church's Articles of Faith and in the Bible. Such assurance is essential to the very being of the Church.

"It has thus been of the greatest importance, in view of what has happened since the invasion of April 9, 1940, that the overseers of the Church have been able to point out that justice has been maintained in accordance with the law of the land. This has been emphasized in several circulars issued by the Norwegian bishops. Thus the Bishop of Oslo, in an extensive pronouncement entitled 'The Temporal and the Eternal,' (July, 1940) followed by each of the bishops in their writings of October and November, stated that 'our laws are being observed and that due respect should be given to all authorities.'

"The attitude of the Church, needless to say, is at all times

*governed by the basic principles outlined above: Norway's
Constitution, the Articles of Faith, and the Bible.*

"Church authorities have hitherto been justified in taking
this viewpoint when advising their ministers and congregations. For Hitler's proclamation of April 24th was in full accord with international law, while the Reichskommissar, in his
talk of June first, declared acceptance of Article 46 of the
Hague Convention which guarantees religious freedom, and
later in his order of September 28th asserted that the independence of the courts should not be touched.

"Recently, however, much serious doubt has arisen concerning the validity of the statements made by the bishops to
their church members. We are faced with the problem of
whether the State and its departments will maintain order and
justice as provided by our Church's Confession of Faith.

"We point to three specific instances which, in substance,
are interwoven and which bear out the contention that acts of
violence, instead of being prevented, are actually condoned.
That the fundamental principles of justice are being broken
down is shown by the following concrete examples:

"1. The systematic rule of terror by the Nazi Storm Troopers.

"2. The resignation of the Supreme Court of Norway.

"3. Interference with the ministers' pledge of silence.

"These accusations are supported by documentary evidence
of which brief résumés are given here:

"1. The attack by Storm Troopers on the Oslo Business
College, November 30th, during which teachers and the direc-
tor were knocked down and severely assaulted, was in itself
bad enough. But the seriousness of the event was increased by
the slogan published that very morning by the official organ of
the Nazi party: 'We shall strike again in such a way that they
shall lose both sight and hearing. Storm troopers, close your
ranks. He who hits us once shall be hit tenfold. This shall be
our watchword.'

"If a nation accepts such a watchword and refuses to uphold

law and order, then it may truly be said that such a nation has abandoned the fundamental principles of law-abiding society. The problem takes on a much more serious aspect because we are here confronted with a series of entirely unprovoked incidents. We call attention to the brutal attack on the chairman of the Students Union at Trondheim on November 29th, and further, to the assault on an office-boy who was kidnapped in an automobile on the night of December 11th, 1940, stripped of his clothes and flogged by Storm Troopers. There have been similar incidents in Oslo and in other towns.

"The gravity of this situation is increased by the fact that so far none of the culprits has been apprehended. On the contrary, the ranking official of 'law and order' issued a decree on December 14th instructing the police not only not to interfere in such incidents, but to give 'active support to the Storm Troopers.' The revolting nature of these single acts of violence is such as to make them a problem concerning the security of society as a whole.

"In addition, there is the circular sent out by the Department of the Interior on December 16th in which all state and municipal employees are ordered actively to support the Storm Troopers. Any refusals will be looked upon as an 'action inimical to the state' and will give rise to drastic punishment.

"If such things should continue systematically, the Church's servants will feel the lack of any basis for guiding the conscience of the people insofar as respect and confidence in law of the land are concerned. Therefore we beg to lay the foregoing documented facts before the head of our Church Department.

"2. The second set of facts which must reluctantly be linked with the above relates to the insecurity which church members feel since the Supreme Court of Norway has abandoned its duties.

"The Supreme Court has asserted that the decree of the Department of Justice of November 14th, whereby the departmental chief is given authority to discharge and appoint jurors, judges and court clerks, constitutes an attack on law and order which is in open conflict with recognized principles and which will lead to the most fateful consequences, since freedom of the courts—which is guaranteed by the Constitution—is of vital importance for security and justice. The very fact that all members of the highest court in the land have found it necessary to resign their duties is one that must needs create within the Church a far-reaching feeling of insecurity with regard to the foundations of law and order in society.

"Since the Confession of Faith of the Church (Augustana § 16) upholds that which is legitimate in the State's actions, and since these articles call upon every Christian to be loyal to the State, the acting head of the Church and Education Department will certainly agree that it is the duty and the right of Church officials to speak up and request information on such serious matters as those just mentioned.

"He will also understand that the seriousness of the situation will not diminish when we emphasize that violence and that a spirit of hate is developing among the people. Not the least important is the way such things affect growing youth. The training of Christian character is by law assigned to church and school, and this constitutes one of the Church's main tasks. Therefore, when the Department of Church and Education, in a bulletin dated November 12th and addressed to all school officials, advises all responsible schoolmen to guarantee upon their honor that they will give positive and active support to every resolution and decree issued by the new authorities,— then, we view the whole matter as approaching a conflict of conscience in the very essence of our profession.

"3. Of the most vital concern to our calling is the newly published order of the police department according to which the professional oath of silence of ministers can be abolished by the police. Our right to professional secrecy is not only guaranteed by law, but has always been a fundamental requirement in the ecclesiastical calling when we minister to sorrow and receive confessions from people in trouble. It is of the utmost importance to the Church that people have full and unqualified confidence in the ministerial oath of silence, as it has been recognized both in Norwegian law and in the Church's decrees throughout all times and in all Christian lands. *To abolish this Magna Carta of the conscience is an attack upon the very heart of the Church.* It is an attack which takes on an especially serious character by the fact that paragraph 5 empowers police to imprison an offending pastor and force him to talk without having been taken before a court of law.

"The above facts, together with other serious happenings which we do not touch upon here, have forced us to send this request for clarification to the Department of Church and Education, in the assurance that the seriousness of our situation will there meet with understanding."

(signed)

EIVIND BERGGRAV J. STÖREN J. MARONI
ANDREAS FLEISCHER HENRIK HILLE G. SKAGESTAD
WOLLERT KROHN-HANSEN

Two weeks later the three bishops Berggrav, Stören and Maroni, on behalf of their colleagues, obtained an audience with the acting Head in order to emphasize the sincerity of the petition and to learn whether it would be given an official reply. The verbal statement of the acting Head did not in any way weaken the arguments presented in the petition.

Three days later the following letter was sent by acting Head Ragnar Skancke to the bishops as of February 1st:

"TO THE COLLEGE OF BISHOPS OF THE
CHURCH OF NORWAY:

"During an interview last October with the Christian Press Bureau, in reply to its questions about the new government's relations to and possible plans for the Church, I stated: 'We have no plans beyond what already has been incorporated in our program; namely, that the basic values of Christianity shall be protected. We hope and believe that the Church and its men have confidence in us. When we say this we mean that we do not intend to touch the Church; it needs peace in order to work in these troubled times.'

"This statement still stands. As far as I can see nothing has happened during the last month which can justify the statement that the State has encroached on the Church's freedom to spread the Gospel in accordance with the will of God, the Church's Articles of Faith and its right to be and act as a congregation.

"The motto of Nasjonal Samling (the Quisling party) is law, justice and peace. The present government intends to live up to this motto to the best of its ability.

"In these times of pioneering and ferment things may happen which are regrettable and which we deplore. That, I think, is understandable. When we have irrefutable proof of such happenings we take action, even in incidents where members of our party are involved. In regard to the allegedly concrete instances of injustice contained in your petition, these will be forwarded to the Department of Justice and the Police Department for their attention.

"As to point $\overline{2}$ in your petition (the resignation of the Supreme Court of Norway) permit me to assure the bishops that even though the judiciary to a certain extent is affected by the new order, the government has not failed to preserve law and order within the land.

"With reference to the Police Department's ruling of December 13th, in regard to the duty of ministers to appear as witnesses, may I state that the oath of silence for ministers of the Church was not absolute before December 13th. There are, as you know, many instances where the oath of silence cannot be observed. This latest ruling must be considered as a new interpretation of the oath of silence, but it is not meant to cancel this oath generally.

"The bishops of the Church may rest assured that they will meet with understanding during the present situation; provided that they in turn show understanding of the new order and the present government.

"The Church is not the only institution in need of peace to fulfill its mission; the State itself needs it. We hereby most sincerely warn the Church against any acts which may increase the unrest of our people. Thoughtless action now may result in serious consequences for the Church. Now as before the Church needs the State in order to be a true Church of the people, and the State needs the Church to maintain law and order and peace. The State and the Church must stand together and serve the people, which they lead. We therefore ask the bishops of the Church and through them all the ministers of the Church of Norway to act in the spirit of good will so that this cooperation may succeed.

"May I at this time request that circular letters from the bishops to ministers or congregations be forwarded in three copies to the Department of Church and Education.

(Signed)   R. SKANCKE."

We feel that our congregations are entitled to see this exchange of letters. Suffice it to say, in regard to the point raised by the acting Head, that the question of our oath of silence was discussed during the above mentioned personal conference. The bishops then brought out the fact that certain suspensions of the oath of silence had been incorporated in the law of Norway for centuries. Such exemptions were legal when a minister felt duty bound to reveal confidential information in order to prevent gross crime which might otherwise have been committed; suspension of the oath of silence was also legal in order to prevent the punishment of innocent persons. We maintained that the revolting new feature of the ruling of December 13th is the fact that the oath of silence may be violated whenever the highest police authorities so decide in the interest of the government, and that ministers will be threatened with imprisonment if they do not break their oath.

The bishops refer further to a written memorandum delivered to the acting Head during a personal conference on January 29, 1941. The text of this follows:

"In our second Article of Faith, all Christians acknowledge Jesus Christ as their sovereign Lord. The importance of this solemn declaration exceeds everything else within our Church. The governmental, the political and the administrative functions do not concern us *per se*. We are involved only when such functions touch our allegiance to Christ. Luther said: 'The secular regime has laws, which do not extend beyond life and property and all concrete things in the world. God will not grant to any one but Himself the right to govern souls.'

"The Acts of God comprise justice, truth and compassion, as conceived by the Church within the structure of the State. The framework of a national community is no concern of the Church. But when it comes to the divine commandments, which are fundamental for all community life, then the Church is duty bound to take a stand. It is useless to wave the Church aside by stating that it is meddling in politics. Luther said in plain words: 'The Church does not become involved in worldly matters when it beseeches the authorities to be obedient to the highest authority, which is God.'

"When the authorities permit acts of violence and injustice, and exert pressure on our souls, then the Church becomes the defender of the people's conscience.

"One single human soul is worth more than the entire world.

"The bishops of the Church have therefore placed on the table of the acting Head certain facts and official communiqués concerning the governmental administration, which, during the last few months, in the view of the Church, are against the law of God. They give the impression that revolutionary conditions are abroad in our land, and that we are not living under the rules of foreign occupation whereby all laws shall be enforced as far as is compatible with the occupation forces.

"The Church is not the State, and the State is not the Church. In wordly matters the State may endeavor to use force

against the Church, but the Church is a spiritual and sovereign entity built on the word of God and on its unity of belief. Despite all its human shortcomings the Church has been given divine authority to spread His law and Gospel among all peoples. *The Church can therefore never be silenced.* Whenever God's commandments are deposed by sin the Church stands unshaken and cannot be directed by any authority of the State.

"From this rock of faith we beseech the authorities to strike out all that is contrary to God's Holy Writ on justice, truth and freedom of conscience, and to build only on the foundation of the divine laws of life.

"We also beseech our people to avoid acts of force and injustice. In an internal struggle all individuals and groups must be guided by this moral law. He who promotes hatred or encourages evil will be judged by God. The Holy Bible says: 'Do not repay evil with evil, but overcome evil with good.'

"Above all of us stands the One who is Lord of our souls. *In our congregations we now perceive a ferment of conscience and we feel it our duty to let the authorities hear clear and loud the voice of the Church."*

(signed)

EIVIND BERGGRAV   J. STÖREN   J. MARONI
ANDREAS FLEISCHER   HENRIK HILLE   G. SKAGESTAD
WOLLERT KROHN-HANSEN

POSTSCRIPT

TO THE BISHOPS' PASTORAL LETTER:

We have received unsolicited communications from nationwide Christian organizations in Norway and from denominations outside of the State Church to the effect that they join the stand taken by the bishops. The statement from these denominations reads as follows:

"The undersigned organizations prompted by the will of

God, by the Church's Articles of Faith and by the conscience of each individual member, hereby express their full agreement with the petition of the bishops." (Signed: The Norwegian Lutheran Home Mission, Oslo; The Norwegian Sunday School League, Oslo; The Western Home Mission, Bergen; The Norwegian Foreign Mission, Stavanger; Norway's Finmark Mission, Trondheim; The Norwegian Seamen's Mission, Bergen; The Santal Mission, Oslo; Norway's Christian Youth League, Oslo; and The Norwegian Lutheran China Mission, Oslo.

The Salvation Army sent the following letter to the bishops:

"The Salvation Army of Norway, guided by our belief and the conscience of our members, hereby approves wholeheartedly the petition which the bishops of the Church of Norway addressed to the acting Minister of the Department of Church and Education."

The bishops received a declaration from the Congress of Dissenting Faiths signed by representatives of its church groups: "The executive board of the Norwegian Congress of Dissenters acting in accordance with the word of God, our Christian faith and the personal conscience of the members of board, hereby subscribes fully to the petition of the bishops of the Church of Norway."

A similar statement has been received from the Philadelphia Congregation of Oslo, signed by its elders.

ANNEXURES

TO THE PETITION OF THE NORWEGIAN BISHOPS TO RAGNAR SKANCKE, THE ACTING SECRETARY OF CHURCH AND EDUCATION, ON JANUARY 15, 1941

1. Statement sent to the Minister of Police, Jonas Lie by the Teachers' Union of the Oslo Business College on the subject of the raid of the *"Hirden"* on November 30, 1940.

2. Report of Paul Hartman, Mayor of Oslo, made to the police regarding the attack on Gunnar Stabel on December 11, 1940.
3. Report of Arne Mo and O. K. Skavlem, students, on the attack on the President of the Student Union on November 29, 1940, submitted to Acting Minister Skancke by the Faculty Council of the Norwegian Technical Institute.
4. Specific orders to the police by the Department of Police, of December 14, 1940.
5. Circular of the Ministry of Interior, of December 16, 1940.
6. Letter from the Supreme Court to the Ministry of Justice, of November 19, 1940.
7. *Augustana*: Paragraph 16, etc.

1

TO THE CHIEF OF POLICE, ACTING MINISTER JONAS LIE.
THE RAIDS OF THE "HIRDEN" ON THE OSLO BUSINESS
COLLEGE ON OCTOBER 21 AND NOVEMBER 30, 1940

On October 21, 1940, the *"Hirden"* forced their way into the courtyard of the College, approached the principal with threats and beat one of the pupils of the institution.

On November 30th the *"Hirden"* once more forced their way in, and prevented the watchman from telephoning for help from the police. On this occasion they entered one of the classrooms during a class and attacked the pupils, who were mauled in the presence of their teacher. The *"Hirden"* used as weapons tables and chairs of iron, throwing them at the students. Ordinary wooden chairs they also threw; and Gundersen, a member of the *"Hirden"*, had a length of rubber hose.

On the same occasion the teacher of the class was knocked down; afterward they attacked the principal, the inspector and another teacher, beating them and inflicting rather serious injuries.

For a specific description of the injuries, we refer you to the statement drawn up by Gunnar Johnson, and moreover to the police report.

On an earlier occasion one of the *"Hirden"* asked questions about *"Nasjonal Samling,"* questions which several teachers of the school cannot but regard as threats.

In regard to the occurrences of November 30th, what made the greatest impression on the teachers was the fact that the police are taking no steps against the *"Hirden"* and have made no attempt to prevent a recurrence of these acts of violence at the school.

Respectfully submitted,

THE MANAGEMENT OF THE TEACHERS' UNION
OF THE OSLO BUSINESS COLLEGE

MADS BOHN   B. KROGH JOHANSSEN

Oslo, December 3, 1940

2

COMMUNE OF OSLO
REGISTRY OF POPULATION AND BUREAU OF STATISTICS

I take the liberty of giving the following information: Gunnar Stabel, a volunteer worker in the Registry of Population, left the office on Wednesday the 11th of this month at his usual hour, 3:45 P. M. When he came to the room on the street floor by the entrance in the right tower, two persons there stopped him, showing an unusual interest in him. One even seized hold of his coat sleeve. Stabel paid no attention, but continued on his way out. When he opened the door, two persons in the uniform of *"Hirden"* suddenly appeared, grasped his arms and, before he could call for help or resist, shoved him into an automobile that stood at the edge of the sidewalk in front of the City Hall. In addition to Stabel, there were in the auto the two *"Hirden"* and the two persons in civilian clothes who had approached him in the City Hall.

Immediately the auto started off, with one of the civilians as chauffeur; then it went to the *"Hirdenheim"* headquarters on Björn Farmann Street.

Here Stabel was taken at once to the cellar, where one of the two *"Hirden"* began to cross-question him and struck him from ten to fifteen times with a strap. The pretext for the abduction and the beating of Stabel was the fact that Stabel was said to have been seen on Monday wearing a ribbon in his lapel. In the course of the scene in the cellar Stabel declared that the ribbon was a sign of national unity and of the hope that the country might again be free. Stabel was also forced to give the name of the person who had given him the idea for the ribbon. . . . On the same afternoon Stabel's brother reported this attack to the police.

Gunnar Stabel was born November 22, 1924; hence he has only recently completed his sixteenth year.

ARVID MESSEL

Oslo, December 13, 1940

This report was sent to the Preliminary Board of the Oslo City Administration; at the same time I informed the President of the Precinct of the affair, and notified the Department of Police, referring to the letter of the President to these same authorities in the matter of the Steinar Rydland case.

PAUL HARTMAN

Oslo, December 13, 1940   MAYOR

3

REPORT OF THE EPISODE IN THE STUDENTS UNION, FRIDAY, NOVEMBER 29, 1940, DRAWN UP BY TWO STUDENT WITNESSES

Trondheim, November 29, 1940

After luncheon we were sitting as usual in the Clubroom, drinking coffee and reading newspapers.

At about a quarter to three the doors were opened violently, and a Leader of the *"Hirden"* came in swinging his rubber club, and shouted:

"Is Holtermann here?"

When no one answered, he said, "Can't you open your mouths?"

Then he went out; when we followed a moment later we witnessed the following scene:

We saw the President of the Union, Holtermann, being led down the corridor by two *"Hirden,"* who held his bound hands behind him. A third *"Hird"* had forcibly seized his shoulder.

About fifteen *"Hirden"* were now present, some not in uniform.

Holtermann was placed before the window of the manager's office, held fast by two *"Hirden."* A *"Hird"* asked Holtermann whether he was willing to post certain placards. Holtermann refused. The Leader then gave the order for the beating to begin.

Holtermann was struck in the face until he fell to the ground. When he had got up on his feet again, the Leader repeated the question, but Holtermann refused once more. He was not willing to post any placards.

Then the Leader ordered the students to go back to the Clubroom or into the dining hall. Part of the students obeyed this command, but the others were passive and did not speak.

The Leader whistled and the *"Hirden"* went off. Some minutes later the Norwegian police came, received information about the occurrence from the students and took down a written report.

ARNE MO   O. K. SKAVLEM

4

CIRCULAR OF THE DEPARTMENT OF POLICE, OF DEC. 14, 1940

The new National Government, which came to power September 25th of this year, is based on two points:

1. The road to the restoration of Norway's freedom and independence leads through the "Nasjonal Samling."
2. "Nasjonal Samling" is the only legal, governmental party.

The employees and officials of the police must draw the consequences from these facts and must have them before their eyes constantly in the performance of their duty. It is desirable that they become members of "Nasjonal Samling" in the largest numbers possible. The present struggle to rally the people demands the full and entire cooperation of the police; it is important for the future of our police that all who are active in the work of the police should understand this fact. Passive loyalty is not enough. It is required that the police stand up for the New Order with their whole power. The old conception that a policeman should be neutral and should not have to join any political party, has lost its validity because only one national and legal party exists and that is the governmental party.

The *"Hirden"* are the political soldiers of the "Nasjonal Samling" and must be strongly supported in their struggle to put the ideas of "Nasjonal Samling" into effect. A good relationship and a real collaboration must be established between the police and the *"Hirden."* Naturally it must not occur that a member of the *"Hirden"* be arrested by the police, except if he has committed a *crime*. If the *"Hirden"* or any members of "Nasjonal Samling" are insulted or exposed to terrorism, their answer is a direct action against the attackers—a circumstance which is recognized as free, on principle, from punishment in Paragraph 228, third Section of the Penal Code. The police must actively join the *"Hirden"* in such cases.

If the police finds for any reason grounds for a complaint of the behavior of the *"Hirden,"* these complaints are submitted to the Police Department, which then has to discuss the question with the national Leader of the *"Hirden."*

At the assemblies of "Nasjonal Samling," the *"Hirden"* functions to preserve order in the hall and at the entrance, and not the police, in such towns as have an established division of the *"Hirden."*

It is requested that all officials be instructed in conformity with this circular.

5

FROM THE MINISTRY OF THE INTERIOR

"Nasjonal Samling" is fighting for Norway's freedom and independence.

At the behest of the Fuehrer of Germany, Reichschancellor Adolf Hitler, on September 25, 1940, Reichskommissar Terboven proclaimed:

"Only 'Nasjonal Samling' shows the way to Norway's freedom and independence."

"Nasjonal Samling" is the governmental party in Norway. Other parties do not exist. For this reason all those who are employed in the service of the country must work actively for the success of "Nasjonal Samling."

Everyone who is employed in the Ministry of the Interior, or in one of its subdivisions of whatever sort, even in the municipal subdivisions, is exhorted to support positively in every way "Nasjonal Samling" and all its organized sections, like the Party, the Women's Group, the Youth Group and the *"Hirden,"* and to cooperate with all his strength in its endeavors, so that the goals of the Movement may be quickly and effectively promoted in the best interests of the whole people and of the land.

All employees of the Ministry of the Interior or of the institutions working under it are responsible for carrying out the above commands.

The slightest disposition towards doubt is regarded as an action hostile to the state.

From now on drastic punishment will be executed on every enemy of the people.

Oslo, December 1, 1940.　　　　　　　　　　　HAGELIN

6

FROM THE SUPREME COURT TO THE MINISTRY OF JUSTICE

On November 14, 1940, the Ministry of Justice issued an order that, among other things, gives the Acting Minister the right to discharge and to appoint court clerks, as well as to subsidize elected magistrates, judges and barristers, and to appoint others.

This order holds true both for civil cases and for criminal cases. It gives the Acting Minister of Justice the opportunity of meddling in the personnel of a court of justice in a way that openly contradicts the principles on which our judiciary system is founded.

The order exceeds the limits of the power of an Acting Minister, the representative of an occupying nation, according to the Fourth Hague Convention of 1909 and its regulation for war on land, in particular Article 43, according to which the occupying Power "shall respect the laws valid in the land as far as there are not absolute hindrances to that principle." The order is also not included in the authority given to the Acting Minister in Paragraph 3 of the Order of the Reichskommissar of April 24, 1940, which declares that the law hitherto in effect shall have legal force as long as it is compatible with the Power in occupation.

The independence of a court of justice has been established in the Constitution, and, in agreement with international law, was expressly recognized by the order of the Reichskommissar, Paragraph 5, on September 28, 1940. The maintenance of this independence is of fundamental importance for the security of justice. Should this order be put into effect, the consequences for the continuance of justice would be fatal.

As the highest representative of the judicial authorities of the Kingdom, the Supreme Court (since resigned from office) must request that this order be not executed.

A copy of this letter is being sent to the Reichskommissar for the Occupied Norwegian Territories.

PAAL BERG	JOHN RIEVERTZ	THOMAS BONNEVIE
THOMAS BOYE	EINAR HANSEN	HENRY LARSSEN
U. A. MOTZFELDT	E. ALTEN	A. T. NÄSS
F. SCHJELDERUP	SVEND EVENSEN	HELGE KLÄSTAD
JACOB AARS	SVERRE GRETTE	EMIL STANG

SIGURD FOUGNER   ERIK SOLEM

Oslo, November 19, 1940.

7

AUGUSTANA, PARAGRAPH 16, reads as follows:

De rebus civilibus docent, quod legitimae ordinationes civiles sint bona opera Dei, quod christianis liceat gerere magistratus, exercere iudicia, iudicare res ex imperatoriis et aliis praesentibus legibus, supplicia iure constituere, iure bellare, militare, lege contrahere, tenere proprium, ius iurandum postulantibus magistratibus dare, ducere uxorem, nubere.

They teach in regard to affairs of state that legitimate measures of government are works pleasing to God, that it is permitted to Christians to hold office, to exercise judicial activity, to pass judgments on the basis of the laws of the government and other laws in effect in the land, to establish lawful punishments, to wage justified wars, to perform military service, to carry on business within the law, to hold property, to depose oaths at the demand of officials, to marry and to live in marriage.

COMMENTARY OF PROFESSOR AHLTHAUS:

The State, that is government in the form of the law, is, according to the teachings of Luther, an ordinance of God, although it has come into existence and is administered everywhere by men; through this His ordinance God preserves humanity in a world of sin and conflict from chaos and makes life in a community possible. The fundamental task of the State is therefore the administration of justice.

THE FOUNDATIONS OF THE CHURCH

A CONFESSION AND A DECLARATION

Easter Eve, 1942.

The present position of the Norwegian Church has forced the clergy to present clearly their confession and declaration on the Foundations of the Church.

Much has already been said in the letters sent by the bishops to the ministers and congregations during the last year, most recently in the circular about the *Church's Order* and in the letter about the *Education of the Children* (February 14, 1942), and in the expert pronouncement by the two theological faculties on February 24th and 27th. We would also refer to the *Pastoral Letter* of last February, (1941) a document which was supported by all the Christian organizations and free Christian communities in Norway and which thereby became a common confession.

The most significant facts of today have been set down in the following six main paragraphs regarding our confession on the foundations of the Church.

I. REGARDING THE FREEDOM OF GOD'S WORD AND OUR OBLIGATION TO THE WORD

We Confess:

that the Holy Writings are the only foundations and guide for Christian teaching and life, and we are firmly convinced that the Evangelical Lutheran confession is the true and proper guide in the question of faith.

We therefore declare that it is our highest duty towards God and humanity to preach all of God's Word, wholly and fearlessly, for discipline and encouragement; and the whole of God's message, for life and salvation, without regard to whom it might annoy. Here we are acting under God's orders.

The servants of the Church, therefore, are not able to accept directives from outside the Church order about how God's Word should be preached in a certain situation. The free preaching of the Gospel shall be God's salt in the life of the people. Nor can any worldly power or authority make conditions on which alone permission is given to carry out Christian work or serve as preacher, which are not approved by the Church. It is a serious blow to the free life of God's Word when that happens. See the letter from the Ministry of Church Affairs, February 10, 1942, where it is stated: "Where the church and organization *recognize Nasjonal Samling and the New Order* . . . the Party will do nothing to hinder Christian work . . .", or the public statement by the secretary of the Ministry on December 1, 1941, according to which the appointment of ministers to offices in the Norwegian Evangelical Church depends on the minister's relation to worldly and political questions.

We confess the freedom of God's Word and our obligation to this Word.

II. REGARDING THE CHURCH AND THE ORDINATION

We Confess:

The Church is an association of believers, where the Gospel is preached correctly and the sacraments administered rightly (Augustana article 7.) Our Lord and Saviour has himself founded his Church and it can never become the organ of any worldly power. The Church has Christ as its master. The Christian congregation must be allowed to gather freely in

God's House, and no one can justly hinder them in so doing.

With the Bible and confession we assert that Christ himself has appointed servants in His Church—with special vocations—evangelists, teachers, priests. In the manner of the apostles, the Church has its method of initiating these servants in the calling. (Ephesians IV:11; I Corinthians XII:28; Acts XIII:2).

For nine hundred years the *ordination* in our Norwegian Church has been an initiation based on the Scriptures. It is an independent and unrelinquishable link in a proper summoning to service in the Church. This spiritual act of authorization is carried out by the Inspector of the Church who for that purpose has received the Church's vocation, authority and initiation; and the sacred ceremony is performed in Divine Service with prayer and laying on of the hands.

The ordination is essentially a *call for life,* to carry out God's work amongst the congregation as far as strength and ability allow. The sacred nature of this work can be destroyed by personal failure, faithlessness, or other sin. But the holy judgment in such serious cases must be passed with due observation of the laws of the spirit of and of justice, which alone can safeguard the individual against injustice and the Church against unworthy servants.

The Church, therefore, finds it intolerable that any ruler should, for political and worldly reasons, not only deny an ordained man his office, but also his commission to work with the Word and Sacrament, and take away his right to wear the clerical robes which belong to the Church. The Church feels it as a blow at the very altar when the Church's ministers are arbitrarily deprived of the right and duty consequent upon the ordination.

We acknowledge the rock of the faithful—Jesus Christ—and the independence and rights of the Biblical initiation in relation to all external considerations. Every minister must be faithful to his ordination pledge, and obey God more than man.

III. REGARDING THE SACRED SOLIDARITY OF THE CHURCH

We confess:

In the Church, which in the Holy Writ is called the body of Christ, there are many duties and branches of work. As the Epistle to the Corinthians says: "The Body has many limbs but is still one body."—"If one limb suffers, suffer the other limbs as well." (I Cor. XII). This expresses for all times the Christian solidarity in life and in suffering.

Not only the servants of the Word—laymen and theologians—but all who in their own calling work according to God's will, belong to the Church's body in Norway. If worldly powers interfere and try to injure the foundations of the Christian school, the Christian home, the Christian voluntary work, or the Christian social work, the whole Church and each of its limbs will suffer.

If a person is persecuted and hounded because of his beliefs, and is unable to take recourse to the law, the Church, as keeper of the conscience, must support the persecuted. In our Church Prayer we pray: "Give strength to those who suffer for the righteousness' sake."

A true Evangelical Church must, therefore, oppose all coercion of the conscience and cannot remain unconcerned when today particular members and servants are being plucked out and allowed to suffer for considered views which all their colleagues share. In such ways Christ's body is injured, and the sacred solidarity sinned against.

We acknowledge the fellowship of all the members of the Church and Jesus Christ.

IV. Regarding the Rights and Duties of the Parents
and the Church in the Education of
the Children

We declare:

Every Christian father and mother has the duty and the
right to rear his or her child in the Christian faith for a Christian life.

God's Word says: "You shall love the Lord, your God, with
all your heart and with all your soul and with all your might.
You must keep these words in your heart and impress them
on your children." (Deut. VI:5–7.) The Holy Writ says to the
children: "Obey your parents in the Lord, for this is right."
(Ephesians VI).

On this Biblical basis, the Norwegian Constitution, Article
2, reads: "The Evangelical Lutheran religion remains the public religion of the State. Those inhabitants who profess this
religion are obliged to bring up their children in the same."

Through the baptism the Church has received the parents'
yes to the effect that they will follow this obligation. During
the laying of hands on the child's head the minister declares
that it is "the almighty God, our Lord Jesus Christ's father,
who has made you His child and received you into His believ-
ing flock." The Christian education of the child is therefore
the *concern of the whole Church,* together with the Christian
school and the Christian home.

The Church would be failing in its obligation and responsibility for Christian training if it simply looked on whilst a
worldly authority organized the children's and people's moral
training independently of the Christian view. One must not
try to force parents and teachers, against their own wish, to
hand over their children to educators who want to "revolution-
ize their spirit" and infect them with a "new moral view"
which seems foreign in relation to Christendom.

V. About the Proper Relation of the Christians and the Church to the Authorities

We declare:

Our Church's confession clearly distinguishes between two orders or regimes: the worldly State and the spiritual Church. It is God's will that these two regimes shall not mix. Both shall—in their own way—serve God through the people.

They both have their clear vocation from God.

It is the Church's vocation to administer the eternal blessings, and to let the light of God's word fall over all human relationships.

Regarding the State's vocation, our confession states that the State has nothing to do with the soul, but shall "defend the body and physical things *against manifest wrongs* and hold the people in check in order to maintain civil *justice and peace.* (Augustana, art. 28.)

We, therefore, profess that it is a sin against God, who is the Lord and the supreme authority over all orders, for one kind of regime to try to assume authority over the other. The Church does not want to become master over the State in temporal matters. That would be a violation of God's arrangement. In the same way, it is a sin against God if the State begins to tyrannize over the soul and tries to dictate what men should believe, consider and know as their spiritual duties. Because if the State tries to coerce and bind the soul in matters of conviction, nothing will come of it but spiritual suffering, injustice and persecution. The judgments in God's Word will then bear force: where the State forsakes justice, it is no longer God's instrument but a demoniacal power (St. Luke IV:6; St. John XIV:30). The foregoing outlines the proper obedience which the Christians should show towards the State, and also the limits to this obedience.

A just authority is a gift of grace from God and we declare together with the *apostle* that on *grounds of conscience* we promise to obey such an authority in all temporal matters. But the words: on the *grounds of conscience* mean that we obey this authority *because of God,* and that we must therefore obey God more than man. The apostle has explained how to recognize this just authority. A just authority is *not afraid of a good deed,* but of a bad deed.

When, therefore, an authority becomes afraid of souls which follow God's way, this authority is no longer an authority according to God's will, and it becomes the Church's duty to God and man to let such an authority hear the word of truth. As the Scriptures say: "Son of man, I have made you keeper, and when you hear a word from my mouth, then you must warn them." (Ezekiel III:17 ff.)

The following words of Luther are also applicable: "The worldly authority shall not rule over the conscience." "When the worldly authority wants to interfere in the spiritual regime and make the conscience captive, where God alone will sit and govern, it must not be obeyed." (See W.A. 12,334.)

On the basis of writing and confession, the Church must, therefore, take exception to those instances where totalitarian demands are made to rule over the conscience and to deny the right to test everything on the foundations of God's Word according to the Christian conscience. The Church, therefore, regards it as opposed to God's order when it is asserted that the worldly power shall have "the highest *authority* and the *greatest* right over each single citizen," (the Ministry for Church Affairs' letter of February 17, 1942), which means that the conscience will not have an opportunity to judge the duty of obedience to the worldly authority in the light of God's Word. (See Minister Lunde's article, March 15, 1942.)

We acknowledge the obedience which the Bible demands towards authority in all temporal matters.

VI. Regarding the State Church

We declare:

According to the Norwegian Constitution and laws the State has certain directive and regulative authority in Church affairs. This does not mean that the State shall dominate the Church with the semblances of power for State or political considerations. The arrangement for a State Church has come about simply because the State has said that it will serve the cause of the Church and defend the Christian faith. Therefore, according to the Constitution, the State, too, has its obligations to the Scriptures and the Church's confession. The Church is therefore bound to be deeply disturbed when a man who is to administrate over the Church publicly declares: "It is quite true that the things of this world are governed by Providence or *destiny.*" (Minister President Quisling's speech on New Year's Eve, see *Aftenposten* for January 2nd.) The State organs can only properly play their part in the Church administration when they work for the proper teaching of the Gospel and the edification of the congregations.

But even though our Church is thus connected with the State, it is still, in its capacity of Jesus Christ's Church, supreme and spiritually free in all God's affairs. The State can never become a Church. In its Church administration it must co-operate with the Church authorities and support the character of the Church as a Confessional Church.

This also applies in the economic field. In a condition of temporal existence it is necessary to use temporal means to further the propagation of the *Word* and the *edification of the Congregation.* That is why Church servants have their salaries and the congregations their churches. The property of the Church does not belong to the State. It belongs to the continuously functioning Christian Church and people. The assets and property of the Church shall serve the Gospel and the congregation's cause and no other. The State organs are managers of a large part of these assets. But a manager must be reliable.

We maintain the spiritual freedom of Jesus Christ's Church also whilst working with a government which manages and protects the Church according to God's word and the Confession.

IN SHORT

What has happened in Norway since September 25, 1940, and especially since February 1, 1942, has forced us to present this, our Confession, about the foundations of the Church.

As long as the above-named conditions remain and are developed by further encroachments, the Church and its servants will be obliged to live and act according to their obligations to God's Word and their Confession and take all the consequences which may follow.

The Evangelical Lutheran Church is today, as it has been for generations before us, our spiritual fatherland in Norway.

We ordained men in . . . parish, deanery or bishopric subscribe with free conviction to the foregoing Confession on the *Foundations of the Church,* and—in so far as we have a position in the State Church—declare that we herewith, for reasons of conscience, lay down our offices, but intend to continue to do all the work and services in our flock which can be done by a non-official in keeping with the Holy Writ, the Church's Confession, and the Service Book of the Norwegian Church.

Similar declarations from individual ministers and congregation councils, bishopric councils, free unions, etc.

The whole declaration is to be read in its entirety to the congregation on the first preaching Sunday, i.e., generally Easter Day; and should be sent directly to the Minister of Church Affairs.

Report of support and declaration should be sent to the nearest clerical superior.